To Run The Race
St. Paul's Second Letter to Timothy

TO RUN THE RACE
ST. PAUL'S SECOND LETTER TO TIMOTHY

Earl F. Palmer

To Stanley with good memories

[signature]

R
Regent College Publishing
www.regentpublishing.com

Published 2014 by Regent College Publishing

Regent College Publishing
5800 University Boulevard, Vancouver, BC V6T 2E4 Canada
Web: www.regentpublishing.com
E-mail: info@regentpublishing.com

Regent College Publishing is an imprint of the Regent Bookstore <www.regentbookstore.com>. Views expressed in works published by Regent College Publishing are those of the author and do not necessarily represent the official position of Regent College <www.regent-college.edu>.

ISBN 978-1-57383-519-0

Cataloguing in Publication information is on file at Library and Archives Canada.

CONTENTS

I dedicate this commentary first to my wife, Shirley

And to Barbara Dan and Howard E. Butt Jr.

And also to you who have been teammates at
Earl Palmer Ministries since our founding in 2008:
Tony Whatley, Scott Hardman, Dick Greiling,
Ken Pyle, Paul Lange, Jackson Chao,
Susan Hutchison, Dan Wilson,
Gordon Stephenson, George Nethercutt,
Sue Nixon and Frank Haas

And Dick Staub at Kindlings Muse

And the Word and Worship team:
Sue Nixon, Walt Wagner, Heather Whitney, Dale
Roth, Brian Coon, Toma Morita and Kay Broweleit

And my Study Assistants at EPM:
Kurt Heineman 2008-09
Daniel Triller 2009-10
Roderick Gellner 2010-11
John Sittser 2011-12
Dexter Kearney 2012-13
Chris Thurton 2013-14
Gray Segars 2014-present

When I think of Paul and his letter to a young friend, I have in mind our children: Anne and Greg, Jon and Kara Diane, Elizabeth and Eric – and our eight grandchildren, aged 17 to 4, Sarah, Kate, Drew, Peter, Emma, Tommy, Emily, and Abraham. May all who read this book find names that remind us of our own in Paul's warmhearted letter to Timothy.

PREFACE

This final letter of St. Paul is a very special book for me. Everything about II Timothy is interesting: the people we meet in its pages, the historic events of its time of writing, and best of all, the message Paul shares. It was written after the mid-point of the first century, during the harsh persecution of Christians during and following the fire at Rome in 64 CE (AD). Nero is emperor, but Paul dares to write about his faith. Paul's trust in Jesus Christ is shared not only with the young friend named Timothy, who receives this letter, but also with all who have read this letter since then. Paul does not talk down to the young man, but writes like a coach to a teammate: He encourages Timothy to trust in the durability and contagious relevance of the good news of the gospel to change people's lives, even those caught up in confusion or danger. This is a letter of amazing grace for each of us as men and women, young and old who are mid-story in the journey of our own lives. We need Paul's letter too, just as much as a first-century reader named Timothy, who first opened its pages.

I have had the privilege of teaching from Paul's second letter to Timothy at New College Berkeley in 2012, a Laity Lodge Weekend in Texas 2013, and in the four great churches of my life, where at numerous times as a pastor I also had this privilege: University Presbyterian Church Seattle, Union Church of Manila, First Presbyterian Church of Berkeley, and the National Presbyterian Church in Washington D.C.

Since 2008, I have been Pastor at Large with Earl Palmer Ministries in Seattle and during this time, I have written this commentary. I want to thank my editors at Regent College Press and two of my study assistants, Dexter Kearney and Chris Thurton, who have aided me in the preparation of this commentary. I especially am grateful to Kathy Tyers who edited my manuscript and also Caroline Ahn, Robert Hand, Rebecca Pruitt, and Bill Reimer.

A special thank you goes to my wife, Shirley, who has been my strongest and most encouraging inspiration not only to me as a pastor and writer but as a husband, father, and grandfather.

Earl F. Palmer
Seattle, Washington

1

PAUL, THE MAN OF TARSUS

Who is this man who writes letters to Timothy? Can we trace the pathways of his life? What would he be like if we met him? His city, Tarsus, was well known as a city of philosophy in the first century—especially within the Greek world—because of Zeno, the father of stoicism. Paul's family was Jewish but aristocratic and privileged. He was a Roman citizen by birth, and on one occasion that we know of because of Luke's account, his family status helped him survive a small-scale but determined personal attack. When Paul made his second visit to Jerusalem as an apostle of Christ, rumors had spread in Jerusalem that he had brought with him a Greek named Trophimus, a native of Ephesus, and had entered the temple with this man (Acts 21). Though probably untrue, these rumors resulted in a riot, which became more intense when Paul tried to speak to the crowd that gathered. He endeavored to argue that the hope of Abraham, Moses, and David should be shared worldwide, even including the non-Jewish world. These words inflamed his Jerusalem listeners. When the crowd rioted, the confusion endangered Paul's safety. At this point the Roman legate in Jerusalem, Claudius Lysias, rescued Paul from the angry crowd, but he sent Paul to the palace of the high priest for interrogation (Acts 23).

Paul learned that a group of forty antagonists had plotted an ambush to take place the following day, during the scheduled transfer of the apostle for a second hearing before the high priest. These men vowed that they would not eat or drink until they had killed him. When Paul heard of the plot, he asked his sister's son to inform the legate of this conspiracy. It was fortunate for Paul that his family had that kind of access to a Roman official. Because of this, the legate sent Paul at midnight with a full military escort from Jerusalem to Caesarea on the Mediterranean coast, where the Roman governor Felix was staying (Acts 23:33). Paul's life was spared, and forty marauders perhaps died of dehydration or at least suffered the collective nervous breakdown of embarrassment at their failure to rub out the man they felt had insulted their intense nationalism.

Paul was not an apostle of Jesus earlier in his life. He was, in fact, a religious extremist who was determined to destroy the message and the messengers of the good news about Jesus. He had been trained as a Pharisee, the lay movement in first-century Judaism that had its roots in the revolt of Judas Maccabeus in 150 BCE. His teacher was Gamaliel, the pupil of the great Rabbi Hillel. These two rabbis represented the moderate wing of the Pharisee movement (Acts 5:33-39). But somehow Saul of Tarsus had moved away from the wise moderation of the Hillel group of rabbis, toward the hardline faction that saw Jesus' followers as a serious threat to the tradition of law and prophets, and of their highly nationalistic kingdom hopes. Saul is first identified to us by Luke, the writer of the book of Acts, as a man present at the brutal and illegal mob stoning of the young deacon in the early church, Stephen. Luke tells us that young Saul was consenting to the murder of Stephen (Acts 8).

Some thirty-plus years later, this same man—now named Paul—would write a letter to a young man named Timothy, who was likely the age of Stephen at the time of his death. Throughout Paul's life, he never forgets the meanness he displayed and the guilt of his own part in that tragedy (note Paul's self-description in Galatians 1:13). However, an amazing interruption of sheer grace changed everything in his life. The same writer who tells of the death of Stephen tells us of that interruption.

PAUL, THE MAN OF TARSUS

On a road not far from Damascus, soon after the events of Mount Calvary and the reports of the empty grave, Saul—the angry religious hardliner—meets Jesus of Nazareth, who was crucified at the order of the Roman governor Pontius Pilate. A sudden light blinds Saul at midday. Jesus speaks. "Saul, Saul, why do you persecute me? It hurts you, doesn't it, to kick against the stationary goads" (Acts 9; 22:6; 26:14).

He asks, "Who are you, Lord?"
Jesus replies, "I am Jesus, whom you are persecuting."
Saul answers with one more question. "What should
    I do, Lord?"
"Go to Damascus, and you will find out."

Paul has made three discoveries: First, that Jesus Christ is alive. Second, that Jesus knows who he is and what he has done, and he does not intend to write off Saul as a terrorist. We do not hear the severe word of judgment that we would expect (and he would expect), but instead words that sound like a shepherd or pastor looking for a lost and wayward sheep: "You hurt, don't you Saul?" His third discovery follows his own response, "Lord, what will you have me do?" He is told, "Go to Damascus and you will find out." His story is not over but at a new beginning place. From Luke's three narratives of this event, we know that at Damascus Paul is healed of his temporary noonday blindness, he is fed, and he is baptized as the sign and seal of the fulfillment of Christ's finding grace in his life. Saul is then a believer—his journey toward healing is begun, and he experiences assurance of his own forgiveness. Two events converge in Saul's redemption: First is the mysterious noontime individual discovery, but the second is his experience in Damascus, of the believers who feed and baptize him.

Because of this remarkable encounter on the road and the surprise of assurance among the small, persecuted Damascus band of believers, Saul will always be marked first of all as a man caught off guard by Jesus the Living Savior, and second as a man who will love and be grateful for the band of believers called the Church. These two marks will always go together for Paul, as a man in Christ and as a man of the people who believe in Christ. His message will always be centered on the Lord Jesus, and his heart and strategy will always seek to encourage and build up those who believe in the same Lord.

This event impresses us in two ways. First, we are confronted by the simplicity of what lies at the center. It is Jesus himself who wins those who will become his followers. Jesus is the one who finds us, the one man who takes

on himself all punishment and persecution at the place
called Mount Calvary, the one man who dies the death
we all must face ourselves, the one man who disarms the
evil that destroys and holds us captive. Jesus is the one
man who identifies himself with us and for us, the one
man who heals even the wounds we inflict on ourselves
as we try to kick against the stationary grand vertical
markers of the law of God's will. Jesus is the one man
who could not be held by death; he made death inoperative and no longer "the last word." He is the one man
who stands not so much in judgment (though judgment
is his right), but as the one who keeps Saul alive on the
Damascus road for all that will come next.

We are also impressed by another surprise. There is a
suddenness about the noontime encounter, but after that
everything moves at a steady, even apparently slow pace:
"Go to Damascus and find out." St. Augustine explains
this steadying journey of sanctification for Paul the new
believer with two words, *solvitur ambulando*.[1] We discover
the way by walking in the way. Saul is healed and made
whole not only in the mystical breakthrough on the road,
but also at Damascus where he meets the frightened but
caring brothers and sisters. At Damascus he is assured by
the Holy Spirit, in the baptism that ordinary Christians

---

[1] A phrase commonly attributed to St. Augustine.

share in and administer for and to him. Therefore the man Saul, who is the Apostle Paul, will not become a mystic in the solitary tradition of individualistic pietism. In the wisdom of the Lord who encountered Paul on the road, the brothers and sisters of faith at Damascus also play a role in the formation of Paul's Christian character. He is not fed on the road, nor is his eyesight restored on the road, nor is he baptized and settled in the assurance of his own belovedness on the road. These key ingredients of his early discipleship come through the fellowship of the believers in Damascus. At Damascus Saul discovers the Church, and he will love it from then on, though it will take time for them to know and trust him. He will need time, and the other believers will need time. It should not surprise us therefore to discover that when he returns from Damascus, the Christians at Jerusalem advise that he travel to his hometown Tarsus for a time between times. His friends, especially a man named Barnabas, provide a vital linkage for the development and growth in maturity of this young believer. They send him off to Tarsus to spend time in a safe place (Acts 9:30). We know of this "time between times" period in his life from Acts. He also tells us in Galatians of time he spent in Arabia.

We next hear of the man we know as Paul in Acts 11, when Barnabas comes to Tarsus to find him and bring him to Antioch. Barnabas seems to feel that Saul would thrive in Antioch. Paul and Barnabas do teach openly in this city for more than a year. Luke tells us that "they openly preached about the Lord Jesus."

Antioch was the third largest city in the Roman Empire, behind only Rome and Alexandria. It was built around 300 BCE, on an advantageous harbor in the eastern Mediterranean Sea, by one of the generals in the army of Alexander the Great. Nicator Seleucus founded the city and named it for his father Anticius. The streets were handsomely paved, and the buildings were supplied with an efficient underground system for water delivery and sewage. Because of trade advantages, the city was wealthy; the people were spoiled by these easy riches. Antioch's citizens had such a reputation for excessiveness and cynicism that orators and actors were openly and rudely mocked during performances. Added to this, the large red light district in Antioch was so well known in the empire that Roman soldiers were not allowed liberty in large parts of the city.

But it was in this very city that an earnest band of Christians came and shared the hope of the Gospel, and they did it beyond the four walls of the Jewish synagogue. It was here that large numbers of Greeks turned toward the Lord Jesus. Luke also tells us in Acts that it was here that the believers were first called "Christians." The irony of Luke's notation is that the new term was probably used cynically by the crowds as a form of mockery; after all, this ability to make fun of orators was a well-tested skill of the citizens of Antioch. In all likelihood, certain mockers coined the word as an insulting reference to what was in fact the best part of the believer's message: "All these people do is talk about the man Jesus Christ, they are Christians for sure." The word may have first appeared as a joke, but nevertheless even in their joking, they identified what was at the center of the believers' message. They did not humorously call them "Presbyterians" or "Lutherans!" It was and still is the central name, "Christ," who is the living center of the good news that finally won the respect and serious attention of many inhabitants of Antioch. The Gospel is about the man Jesus who is the Christ, and the followers of this man, Jesus of Nazareth, claim all meaning for their lives from him. Antioch's citizens figured this out.

Fyodor Dostoevsky may have had the cynical atmosphere of Antioch in mind when he wrote his novel *The Brothers Karamazov*. Ivan, the middle brother, has travelled to Paris; perhaps it is there that he has become an atheist. He returns home to Russia only to find that his younger teenage brother Alyosha has become a follower of the Russian Orthodox Church, especially devoted to a pious priest named Father Zosima. Ivan invites Alyosha to lunch, and during that famous lunchtime scene he attempts to shock his brother with a scandalous report on the corruption and falsity of Alyosha's Christian superstition, especially the Russian Orthodox Church. After Ivan's long narrative, Alyosha finally speaks. "Yes, I know of the sinfulness of the church, but you see Ivan, we have a Savior Jesus Christ who is able to redeem and heal all such sins...."[2]

Ivan interrupts his younger brother with a fascinating and cynical sentence. "Ah yes, I knew you would drag in Jesus, you Christians always do that." [3] Just as at Antioch, Ivan—though he speaks in what he intends as crude humor—nevertheless has seen the main point after all. It is no surprise that after Ivan's brush-off statement comes the greatest moment in the novel. Ivan says to his brother, "You know, Alyosha...about a year ago I composed a sort of poem. Let me tell you about it."[4] The "Grand Inquisitor" parable follows, where we meet Jesus, who is the one who sets us free.

---

[2] Adaptation of Alyosha and Ivan's conversation from: Fyodor Dostoevsky, *The Karamazov Brothers*, trans. Ignat Avsey (New York: Oxford University Press, 1994), 308.
[3] Ibid.
[4] Ibid.

At Antioch, the believers provide for the Apostle Paul a beginning place for his remarkable ministry, which will take him and his teammates to almost every major city of the Roman Empire. Finally, as a prisoner of that empire, he will arrive in the capital city. In that imprisonment he will write his final letters, and according to the witness of Clement, a late first-century writer, Paul will lose his life in the arena at Rome. Following the fire in Rome in 64 CE during Nero's reign, Clement tells us that Paul was thrown to the lions as part of the Roman persecution of Christians.

The last New Testament prison letter Paul will write is this letter to his young friend Timothy. One more question remains for us, who read Paul's letters and the chapters about him in the book of Acts. What was he like? One feature is universally noted: Paul was intellectually bright. It shows in his use of language, which is always fluent and often poetic. His vocabulary is extensive, so that he is able to find just the right word when he needs it. For example, in Romans 5 when he is seeking to explain the redeeming love of Jesus, who takes our place as the second Adam, he makes use of the relatively complicated word "reconciled" to show that we who are saved by grace are not only set free, "redeemed" toward righteousness, but that we are changed, "reconciled" by the one who can change us.

Paul quotes often from the sacred scriptures of the Hebrew Bible, and though he understands and is fluent in classical Hebrew, he always makes use of the Septuagint, the 100 BCE Greek translation of the Old Testament produced by 70 rabbis in Alexandria. In one instance, he silences a crowd in Jerusalem when he addresses them in Hebrew. They expected to hear Greek, because after Alexander the Great and the Hellenization movement (336 BCE), Greek has increasingly become the major language for communication among the diverse peoples of the Mediterranean world, including first-century Palestine.

Paul is a likeable man, and he makes friends across boundaries that many are unable to cross. We find proof of this as we read the lists of names that appear in his letters. Paul easily relates to slaves, and there are numerous slave names in his lists. He is at ease with privileged citizens of the empire as well, which also becomes clear in the names he notes at the ends of his letters. He is able to make friends with and be befriended by Roman soldiers. At the end of the Philippian letter, he sends greetings from "Those in Caesar's household." These would include soldiers. One notable Roman official is Julius the centurion, who becomes Paul's friend aboard the prison ship that finally breaks apart in heavy seas and goes aground near Malta (Acts 28). Luke tells us that Julius sets the prisoners free in order to save Paul, who has become his friend. Paul also becomes friends with Publius, the chief leader on Malta. This should not be a surprise, since he is able to relate warmly to people across generational boundaries. Paul respects people, and we see that in the way he relates to the young man from Philippi who became a failed missionary because of illness, Epaphroditus (Phil. 2). Epaphroditus must return because of his own illness to his home at Philippi, carrying Paul's letter to the Philippians. Paul honors this young man, along with respectfully honoring the two Philippian women, Euodia and Syntyche, who are having an argument (Phil. 4).

I believe Rembrandt wonderfully captures this thread of kindness in Paul's life in his painting of Paul with parchments opened before him. Paul the intellectual man of ideas is also Paul the letter writer, who makes time to personally keep in touch with his friends.

2

THE BOOK PAUL WROTE

The last New Testament book that Paul wrote is this second letter to his young friend Timothy. Here are some of his words: "Be sure to bring with you the books and especially the parchments that I left at Troas with Carpus, and the coat too. Watch out for Alexander the coppersmith, beware of him... Luke is here with me now, our friend Trophimus is ill at Miletus, I hope Mark can come with you too; do your best to come before winter..." (II Tim. 4). Something about these words won me over to the man who wrote them, and to his friend Timothy too. They are plain words, not too religious, very to the point, practical, and the kind I would expect a friend to write if he knew me well. They happened to be almost the final words from the first-century champion of Christian faith, and they went to a young man he thought of as a son, a borrowed son.

As I read II Timothy I discover that Paul, who was a mentor to Timothy, has become a mentor to people of every generation and time. St. Paul is a borrowable friend. In fact, all of his books have this same knowable and personal atmosphere about them. I can see how a reader of Romans might scan the long list of names in the last chapter of that book for his or her own name.

I am grateful for this connecting, which takes place when we read the New Testament letters even though many centuries separate their stories from ours. But in a strange way, the human stories in New Testament accounts and our human stories are not all that different.

Did Paul actually write this letter to Timothy? Except for the second-century cleric Marcion, all of the early church fathers recognized Paul as author and quoted extensively from his pastoral letters (I & II Timothy, Titus, Philemon). Marcion did not include any of those letters in his own selected New Testament, probably because these books—and large parts of the gospels that he also omitted—strongly challenged key parts of his own special theology.

The tradition of ignoring what does not fit our own ideas is not unique to Marcion. When the Soviet encyclopedia was published in the 1950s, it only included two sentences about Jesus Christ (The N.Y. Times, in its review of the Soviet tome, observed, "This tells us more about the Soviet encyclopedia than it does about Jesus

Christ"). Other religious people have shown us their tendency toward avoidance; for example, Thomas Jefferson—a theist—created his own Jefferson Bible to support the theology he approved. Within the twentieth century, a committee of interpreters in Eugene, Oregon called the "Jesus Seminar" developed a reading guideline that could be used (in their view) for a more enlightened approach to the New Testament gospels. Certain parts were downgraded and others permitted by committee vote.

But the early second-century theologian Polycarp quotes II Timothy as a book by St. Paul, as do Irenaeus and Tertullian. Not only that, but in the second century the New Testament, including the pastorals, was translated into Latin and Syriac. The first orthodox canon, The Muratorian Fragment (ca. 170-200), mentions Paul's letters to seven different churches and then adds these words: "But he wrote one letter to Philemon, and one to Titus, and two to Timothy from affection and love."[1] All this supports the early Church's acceptance of Paul as this book's true author.

The authorship problem for modern interpreters began with Friedrich Schleiermacher in 1807. He suggested that the pastoral letters were written later, by an individual

---

[1]Ralph H. Earle, *The Expositor's Bible Commentary: Ephesians through Philemon* (Grand Rapids: Zondervan, 1978), 346.

or perhaps a committee in a Pauline community, who sought to borrow Paul's authority to undergird their own teaching.

Other interpreters followed Schleiermacher, especially in Germany. The technical science of manuscript dating was not developed until later, and as a result of Schleiermacher's work, many people came to question the Pauline authorship of not only the pastorals but also Ephesians and John's Gospel. Many scholars of that era saw that gospel as a dogmatic teaching document dating from the second or third century, and therefore they did not read it as a serious historical narrative of the life of Jesus of Nazareth.

The most reverent interpreters of this post-Schleiermacher period described the situation as follows: "Considering the immense impact made by the Apostle Paul... it is no wonder that in a later generation there were those who longed for his firm hand upon affairs.... It is better to view all three letters as wholly 'secondary,' i.e. the work of a 'Paulinist' rather than of Paul himself."[2] Another commentator writing in 1960 suggested that a sincere Paulinist wrote at a later date what he really

---

[2]Frederick C. Grant, *Nelson's Bible Commentary: New Testament, Romans-Revelation,* vol. 7 of *Nelson's Bible Commentary* (New York: Nelson, 1962), 222.

believed Paul would have said, had he been still alive.[3] Some interpreters strained to cover all possibilities; e.g. one Catholic interpreter in explaining the mention of the mother, Eunice, and grandmother, Lois, in chapter 1: "The recollection of Timothy's early introduction to the faith and of the tradition of belief going back to his grandmother fits the letter's conception of the church as the household of God."[4] C. K. Barrett put it in the most dramatic way: "The result...was of the highest possible value, for it projected the work and influence of Paul into a new generation, and retained for him his place as Doctor Gentium, the teacher of the Gentile Church in one of the most significant and dangerous periods in its history."[5]

But what if Paul was the actual teacher, and therefore does not need to be journalistically enhanced or have his name borrowed by the "author" of a pseudo-book? Thankfully, the most recent commentators have let the texts speak.

---

[3]A.R.C. Leaney, *The Epistles to Timothy, Titus, and Philemon: Introduction and Commentary* (London: SCM, 1960).

[4]Benjamin Fiore, *Pastoral Epistles: First Timothy, Second Timothy, and Titus*, vol. 12 of *Sacra Pagina Series*, ed. Daniel J. Harrington (Collegeville, MN: Liturgical Press, 2007), 140.

[5]C.K. Barrett, *The Pastoral Epistles: In the New English Bible*, ed. H.F.D. Sparks (Oxford: Clarendon Press, 1963), 17.

Luke Timothy Johnson writes that the air cleared for him when he actually began to teach II Timothy. "It was teaching New Testament introduction at Yale in 1976 that I started to question the pseudonymous authorship position."[6] Therefore he now writes, "These are real rather than fictional letters." The same thing happened for William D. Mounce. In his commentary he challenges modern interpreters, who begin with themes they want to see and then force ancient texts to comply in order to be approved by modern readers and to satisfy modern issues. "There is no legitimate reason that Paul must speak about issues modern scholarship deems to be the core of Pauline thought every time he writes."[7] The Jewish scholar Gabriel Justiprovici, in his book explaining the proper reading of the first five books of the Old Testament, helped me to ask the right questions when I read any part of the Bible. He wisely criticizes the interpreters of the books of Moses, who are often slavishly dominated by their theory of the four strands of documents present in Genesis through Deuteronomy (Elohist, Yahwist, Priestly, Deuteronomist). He writes that the documentary interpreters decided often in advance what J.E.P. and D.

[6]L.T. Johnson, *The First and Second Letters to Timothy,* vol. 35A of *The Anchor Bible Commentaries* (New York: Doubleday, 1999) xi.

[7]William D. Mounce, *Pastoral Epistles,* vol. 46 of *Word Biblical Commentary* (Nashville: Thomas Nelson, 2000), lxxxix.

should have written, and this resulted "in the death of reading; for a book will never draw me out of myself if I only accept as belonging to it what I have already decreed should be there."[8]

One of the best friends of biblical scholarship in regard to both the Old Testament and the New Testament has been the science of manuscript archeology, which has consistently demanded earlier and earlier dates for all of the documents we have for the books called the New Testament. William F. Albright, the most noteworthy of modern archeologists, wrote in a monograph, "We can already say emphatically that there is no longer any solid basis for dating any book of the New Testament after A.D. 80."[9] This means that the most recent manuscript evidence and research has changed everything. It makes the later-writer thesis very hard to cling to. The 1946 discovery at the caves at Qumran of a large library of Old Testament manuscripts, as well as rabbinic commentaries and even pre-first century maps, has been a great aid to Old Testament study. Since all the Qumran documents date from about 100 BCE, the manuscripts help us to

---

[8]Gabriel Josipovici, *The Book of God: A Response to the Bible* (New Haven, CT: Yale University Press, 1988), 15.
[9]William F. Albright, *Recent Discoveries in Bible Lands* (New York: Funk & Wagnalls, 1955), 136.

understand the religious climate at the time just prior to the ministry of our Lord.

Recently in Egypt, the finding at Nag Hammadi of a large Gnostic library from the later second and third centuries has also helped us to understand some of the pressures that were already present upon the first-century Christian Church. We sometimes call these pressures the pre-Gnostic philosophical preferences; they came in from the Greek world, from people raised under the influence of Plato and of most of the Greco-Roman mystery cult religious practices, which were widely observed in the Roman world.

Therefore, Christians like Paul, John, Luke and Timothy needed to share the faith of the gospel toward and into two cultural worlds. First, the good news needed to speak to the first-century Jewish world. The New Testament writers preached to Jewish listeners about the goodness and faithfulness of God revealed in Jesus of Nazareth, who is the fulfillment of ancient Jewish expectation for a father like Abraham, a deliverer and shepherd like Moses, and a king like David. But they also shared good news to the Greek listener. Greek listeners wanted wisdom and spiritual breakthroughs. They wanted to hear of the victory of eternal reality over and above the earthly reality of common physical existence. The challenge for the earliest preachers of the gospel was to stay faithful to the truth and to share it persuasively toward both culture groups. This was the task for every writer in the New Testament.

As II Timothy unfolds, we will watch Paul play his role as an ambassador for Christ to both cultures, and also into yet a third cultural frame of reference—the practical world of the Romans. The success of the Roman military, which won total victory over the whole of the Mediterranean world, combined with the organizational brilliance of Roman government, and this becomes yet another cultural context. These practical and efficient builders of water aqueducts and road bridges, with their systems of political control, were also a people who needed to hear words of grace and truth and to discover a different, profounder power. We know that Paul was able to cross all three of these cultural boundaries to share the good news about Jesus to people who had very little in common with each other, except that they were all human men and women who hoped and feared and needed love and lasting meaning.

Setting the date of this letter is at best a chronologists' guess. We know some dates for certain: the dates of Felix (52-55 CE), and Festus (55-59 CE), the Roman proconsuls to Jerusalem. This would place Paul's arrival in Rome, after the prison ship and the time at Malta, at about 60 CE. Luke tells us of a two-year house arrest, and some have wondered if Paul was released after that for a period of time, perhaps for his hoped-for trip to Spain. We don't know. Clement tells us in his letter at the end of the first century that Paul "travelled as far as the extremity of the West."[10] Is that a reference to Spain? More likely, it is a reference to Rome. One thing is clear: His imprisonment became harsher, because the harshest period of Nero's reign began in the early 60s. Paul's imprisonment was probably in the 60s, during which he wrote his prison letters and finally the second letter to Timothy.

---

[10]James A. Kleist, ed., *The Epistles of St. Clement of Rome and St. Ignatius of Antioch*, vol. 1 of *Ancient Christian Writers* (New York: Newman Press, 1946), 12.

3

REASONS FOR A LETTER LIKE II TIMOTHY

Readers of the New Testament letters always ask one question: Why was this letter written? In other words, what did the writer have in mind as a purpose for writing? The best answer comes from within the content of the letter itself. In the case of II Timothy, at least four purposeful themes become clear when the letter opens up to us. First and of most importance is Paul's desire to encourage his young friend, who probably has been sent out by Paul on his own mission of encouragement to the churches in the Roman provinces of Macedonia and Asia (modern-day Turkey). Paul actually tells the Philippians that Timothy will come to visit them (Phil. 2:19-24). Timothy may have followed that visit by travelling to Ephesus and probably his home city of Lystra, in the large area called Galatia. Paul is an encourager. Throughout II Timothy, this theme of his steady confidence in the goodness and faithfulness of the Lord is

Paul's major message—even in the face of the hardship that all Christian believers are facing throughout the cities of the Roman Empire during this time of stress, especially following the fire in Rome.

A second goal of this letter is to warn Timothy of dangers within the Christian fellowship, especially at those cities where proto-Gnostic influences were present. Gnosticism focused on "spiritual secrets" about Jesus Christ that only a few select and knowing people could understand. Some taught that there was a hidden, new, totally spiritual resurrection now available for "knowing" spiritual leaders. Paul warns against these false teachings, which have caused some first-century Christians to reject the earthiness and concreteness of the Gospel of Jesus. These false teachers advocated a more platonic hope by spiritualizing Jesus himself. Paul, like John in his first letter, warns against this moral and spiritual confusion.

Paul's advice to his young friend is to patiently teach his way through errors that may confront Christians, and to be faithful as an expositor of the biblical texts of sacred scripture that Timothy first learned from his grandmother and mother. Paul promises that over the long journey, the truth of the whole message of the good news of Christ will win out. Timothy needs to trust in that assurance, in the promise and the one who is the promise.

Finally, Paul has personal requests about books at Troas and a coat he left there. He urges Timothy to try and come before winter and not to travel alone, but to bring Mark with him.

4

TIMOTHY

One of the ironies of first-century Christianity is that people in a city like ancient Antioch would become Christian in the first place. They didn't fit the mold. Add to that the fact that the believers in Jesus at Antioch, who were mainly Greek and Roman, would send two of their Jewish members, Barnabas and Paul, to travel considerable distances in order to tell the good news of Jesus to the Roman world. But according to Luke's narrative in the book of Acts, this is what actually happened. These two missionaries and others who traveled with them are commissioned to travel first to Cyprus, and then to the city called Antioch at Pisida, then to Lystra. At Lystra, a strange thing happened. After Paul's healing of a lame man, a crowd of people including a priest of the temple of Zeus shouted praises to Barnabas and Paul, calling them gods. "Barnabas they called Zeus and Paul they called Hermes" (Acts 14:12). What happened next was chaotic. Paul and Barnabas shouted to the crowd that they were not gods but mortals, and before they could tell the good news at the heart of this disclaimer, the confused crowd threw stones at Paul. Fortunately for Paul—and world history—the Christians in Lystra surrounded him and rescued him from the riot. "It is through many persecutions that we must enter the kingdom of God" (Acts 14:22).

Some months later Paul returned to Lystra, this time with Silas (Acts 16:1-5; Luke the beloved physician may have also been present on this part of the journey). At Lystra, they met up with a young man who was the son of a Jewish woman named Eunice. His father was Greek, but we can conclude from the texts that his father was absent or had died, because this young man was being raised by his mother and grandmother. The young man is called a disciple and a man "well spoken of by the believers in Lystra and Iconium." I have wondered if he may have been one of those who helped protect Paul earlier, in the dangerous stoning incident. His name was Timothy.

From this point on in the book of Acts, and in the letters of his mentor-colleague the Apostle Paul, we learn more about Timothy than any other member of the team of St. Paul, the team that takes such a decisive part in the life of the early Christian fellowship. Paul will call him his "son" and his "brother." In St. Paul's letter to the Romans, he will call Timothy "my fellow worker." Timothy is probably the secretary for Paul in writing the Philemon letter as well as the II Corinthian and Colossian letters.

In I Corinthians, Paul tells the Corinthians that if Timothy visits he should be highly respected, for "he is doing the work of the Lord just as I am" (I Cor. 6:10). He tells the Philippians, "I have no one like him… but Timothy's worth you know, how like a son with a father he has served me…" (Phil. 2:20-22). We know that Timothy travelled with Paul throughout Greece and for a period of time was with Paul at Ephesus (Acts 19:22). Then after a time in Macedonia, Paul and Timothy were together in Troas. Paul instructs Timothy to minister with the Christians in Ephesus (I Tim. 1:3). We do not have evidence of Timothy traveling to Jerusalem with Paul in his final visit there, or of his ability to make contact with Paul during Paul's two-year detention at Caesarea during the time of Felix and Festus. But when Paul finally arrives in Rome as a prisoner, Timothy once again appears as Paul's secretary (writer) and as one whom Paul sends as his missionary and pastoral representative to churches at Corinth and Philippi.

This is the young man who now receives the remarkable letter from Paul that we call II Timothy.

5

THE ROMAN WORLD IN THE TIME OF PAUL & THE NEW TESTAMENT

The shrewd Prime Minister Antipater the Nabatean was not Jewish, but he was employed as principal political officer by the remaining Jewish descendants of the Maccabean hero Judas Maccabeus during the years around 80 BCE. Antipater served in Jerusalem during the time of the Roman Empire's spread to the south. He befriended two young Roman military leaders, Marc Anthony and Octavian, as they led Roman soldiers to Egypt after defeating the Seleucids and the remnants of the old Persian Empire in the north. When the territory of Palestine was brought under total Roman control, and because of the recommendation of the two young generals, Julius Caesar rewarded Antipater for his friendship by making him a "friend of Caesar" and granting him extensive gifts of land. When Antipater was assassinated, Julius Caesar named Antipater's son the King of the Jews so that there would be a parallel, but not equal, establishment of governance in the Roman territory of Palestine. This son of Antipater was Herod the Great, who ruled from 37 to 4 BCE. Paul meets Herod's heir, Herod Agrippa II, at the governor's rented palace at Caesarea. That meeting with Festus, along with Herod Agrippa II and his wife Bernice, would have been at or near 55-60 CE. This date would establish Paul's arrival in Rome after Malta at or around 61 or 62. Other, earlier dating markers are also helpful. Luke tells us in Acts 18 of Paul's trial in Corinth before the Roman Proconsul Junius Annaues Gallio (the brother of the philosopher Lucius Annaeus Seneca), who held his position from 41-54 CE.

The early years of the first century were relatively steady and free of turmoil after Julius Caesar's death in 27 BCE. The young general Octavian became Caesar Augustus and reigned from 27 BCE to 14 CE. Our Lord was born during his reign, probably in 4 BCE. Following Caesar Augustus, Caesar Tiberius reigned from 14-37 CE. He was followed by the vicious and insane Gaius Caligula from 37-41 CE. After the assassination of Caligula, Claudius followed with a more stable reign from 41-52 CE, though under Claudius there was an increase in deliberate and official pressure upon the Jewish communities both in Palestine and in the synagogues throughout the cities of the empire, except in Alexandria, where Jews were tolerated. Because of that governmental pressure, Paul would meet up in Corinth with the Jewish couple Prisca and Aquila, who were required to leave Rome. At Corinth, they would become Paul's close friends for the rest of his life.

Unfortunately for Emperor Claudius and his son Britannicus, the emperor married the ambitious Agrippina, who was a distant relative of Caesar Augustus and who was determined to see her own son, who had been adopted by her husband Claudius, become emperor. After the mysterious poisoning of Claudius and his son Britannicus, who should have been his father's successor, the senate confirmed the elevation of 16-year-old Nero Claudius Caesar Drusus Germanicus as emperor.

Nero's first three years were called "golden years" because of the wisdom and moderation of his tutors, the philosopher Seneca and the political leader Burris, but by the time Nero was 19, he seized absolute authority and was determined to be recognized as the greatest of all emperors. Nero's obsession with fame and greatness is evidenced even in Athens, where an inscription has been found on the east side of the Parthenon: "The emperor supreme, Nero Caesar Claudius Augustus Germanicus, son of god." He saw himself as an orator and chariot driver and therefore appeared in oratorical contests and chariot races. In all contests, he always won the competition.

A time of horror and intrigue engulfed the Roman Empire during his tenure, especially following the catastrophic fire of Rome in 64 CE, after which Nero diverted blame for the fire from himself by accusing the Christians of arson. The Roman historian Tacitus, who chronicled the whole reign of Nero, makes it clear that most citizens of Rome suspected Nero himself was responsible for the fire. He had originally planned a controlled fire in a slum area of the city, in order to make space for his grand palace with golden garden and monuments, but apparently it spread throughout the whole city.

A terrible persecution followed the fire of Rome, not only in the capital but in other cities. It is my view that the book of Revelation was written by John on the prison island of Patmos during the later part of Nero's persecution, about 70 CE. Nero himself committed suicide in 68 CE; the Emperor Vespasian continued the punishment of rioters and Jewish nationalists in Jerusalem, culminating in the destruction of that city around 70 CE. I agree with William F. Albright that there is no reason to date any book in the New Testament later than that date. This would place the Johannine books at and around 80 CE.

The letters of Paul are earlier, and according to Clement—the early church father who wrote to the church of Corinth at 96 CE—both St. Paul and St. Peter were killed in the Roman arena, Paul by lions and Peter by crucifixion. The irony of this period of persecution is that it was rooted in the need for an emperor to blame a recognizable minority group for the great fire of Rome.

The fire was intended to clear ground for Nero's ambitious building plans. He was very much like the later tyrant Adolf Hitler, who commissioned his special architect Albert Speer to design and build a vast arena in Nuremburg for the spectacle of the 1939 Nazi Rally. Speer created what he called a cathedral of ice, with hundreds of searchlights that pointed into the sky and surrounded an arena that held a million men and women for the Third Reich's celebrations of triumph. An immense eagle was displayed at the front of the stadium, and thousands of flags with the terrifying swastika of black on red lined every aisle and edge. Hitler was also determined to build the world's largest dome for his planned new capital in Berlin. Nero created a 125-acre golden villa, and a garden with a colossal, 120-foot tall image of himself. Later, between 80 and 90 CE, the Emperor Titus built the Coliseum—seating 50,000 spectators—on the site of Nero's garden. That Coliseum still stands, the most recognizable structure of first-century Rome. It was completed in 90 CE by another emperor, Domitian. It also would be a site of horror, persecution, and death for many Christians.

Mingled with Nero's ambition was a persistent paranoia that caused him to arrange for the assassination of everyone he suspected of hindering his plans. This included not only the Christians, whom he blamed for the fire, but even his early tutors Burris and Seneca, his pregnant wife, and finally his own mother Agrippina—who had killed others to ensure her son's reign. Her words at her own death are famous: "Strike my womb, for it bore Nero."[1] This man ruled as emperor from 54-68 CE, during the life and ministry of St. Paul, who died among other ordinary believers before the lions in Nero's arena.

Today few remember Nero, except with horror and disdain, while the prisoner Paul is remembered and honored: The world's third-largest city, Sao Paulo, is named for him. So is a cathedral in London that withstood the Battle of Britain—St. Paul's Cathedral. A cathedral in his honor stands in Malta near St. Paul Beach, where a Roman prison ship broke apart at sea. Every artist in the Renaissance painted portraits of Paul,

---

[1]Lucius Annaeus Seneca, *Treatises on Providence, On Tranquility of Mind, on Shortness of Life, On Happy Life*, rev. ed., ed. by Bishop John Fletcher Hurst and Henry C. Whiting (New York: American Book Company, 1877), 17.

including—perhaps most notably—Rembrandt. Felix Mendelssohn wrote an unforgettable oratorio called "St. Paul." Christians name our sons for this man, and for his young friend Timothy. We read his letters, because Paul points not to himself but to Jesus, another man who died for others but who won the greatest victory of all time at the cross on a Friday... and three days later, when his tomb lay empty. He is the one who proved that love is a person, and that we can know that person.

It amazes us that when the believers in Christ shared this message of faith, hope, love, and joy with their generation, it would appeal to such a vast company of young and old, Greeks and Jews, women and men, Roman citizens and slaves. The oppressive power of first-century Roman emperors could not destroy or even slow down the person-by-person spread of this good news. When we who live in our century read the letters and gospel narratives of the first century, we gain a greater understanding of this contagious spread of the hope of the gospel, and of the people who were a part of that hope. We who read the New Testament today look for clues to this remarkable social and historical reality.

The scholarly search is one way to read ancient accounts, but another way is to allow ourselves to enter into the New Testament and Old Testament narratives, so that we are changed by the good news of God's love—just as were the men and women we meet in the pages of the Bible. One of those was the young man named Timothy from Lystra, who first met the teacher Paul during a riot.

6

THE TEXT OF II TIMOTHY

II Timothy 1:1-2 Paul, an apostle of Christ Jesus by the will of God, for the sake of the promise of life that is in Christ Jesus, To Timothy, my beloved child: Grace, mercy, and peace from God the Father and Christ Jesus our Lord.

At the very beginning of this letter, Paul describes himself in three ways: First, he is a messenger (apostle) who belongs to Jesus Christ; second, because of the decision of God his task as an apostle is rooted in God's will, and therefore God's intention stands behind the sending of a man like Paul.

The third description shows the goal toward which Paul is a messenger: the promise of life in Christ Jesus. That promise is the noun source of the verb implied in a word like apostle, a "sent one." The verbal action word is mixed with the dynamic and powerful will of God's intention, and all this moves toward the goal that is found in the promise of life for the young man who is to receive this letter.

In most of Paul's letters, since he dictated them to a secretary, there is some clue as to who recorded the text (see Rom. 16:22, II Thess. 3:17). That clue is usually in the letter's opening, as in Philippians and I and II Corinthians. In this letter it may be Eubulus, who is especially noted at the end of the letter, "Eubulus sends greetings to you…" (II Tim. 4:21), or perhaps Luke, since he is mentioned first among the list of names, "Only Luke is with me…" (4:11).

In verse 2 Paul describes Timothy, the one who will receive the letter, as "my beloved child." We know that Timothy is not Paul's biological son, and yet he is like a son to Paul, and therefore he is honored by that description. The relationship word "child" gives us one more clue to the fact that Timothy is young when he receives this letter. Many other clues to his age will be found as the letter unfolds. Also, in I Timothy 4:11 Paul had earlier written to Timothy, "Let no one despise your youth, but set the believers an example in speech and conduct, in love, in faith, in purity."

But Paul adds four more words to describe Timothy: First, he calls him "beloved." This is the word *agape*. Paul called love "the greatest word" in I Corinthians 13. *Agape* in the New Testament is the event word that explains the profound source of the promise of life. The

Apostle John puts it this way: "Here is love, not that we loved God but that he loved us and gave his son to take our place on the cross" (I John 4:10). Paul said it in Romans 5: "God proves his love for us in that while we still were sinners Christ died for us." *Agape* in the New Testament is not theoretical but actual. It is physically concrete; love is the person of Jesus Christ at the cross and in his victory over sin, death, and the power of evil. Timothy is beloved because of Jesus Christ, and at the opening of this book "beloved" becomes a part of his name.

Paul then adds three more words, beginning with "grace." The root for this word in Greek is *chara*, which means joy. "Surprise" is the basic sense of *chara*. In this longer form, *charis*, the word becomes part of the love vocabulary for New Testament writers, meaning "the surprise gift of love that has caught us off guard." We did not expect to be loved, and yet there is the promise of good news in front of our eyes. We are loved by surprise. It is the greatest gift. *Charis* becomes itself the root word for "gift" in the New Testament, *charismata*. Paul will use this word in I Corinthians 12 to explain the surprise of other gifts that we receive from God. When the Greek prefix *eu* is put before *charis*, we have the New Testament word for thanksgiving: "the good surprise gift we give out of gratitude for love." This word, *eucharist*, will become the church's word for the Lord's Supper, the supper of thanksgiving for the surprise sacrifice of Jesus of Nazareth on our behalf.

It is the word *charis* that he adds to his greeting. Timothy is "beloved," and now he hears of the surprise of love that continues to flow toward and through him like a dynamic, surprising river.

Then comes the word "mercy," *eleos*. This word is concrete and definite. It describes specific acts of love. It is the word our Lord used in the parable of the Good Samaritan, in which the Samaritan is described as the one who concretely showed that he cared about the man who fell among robbers. Our Lord makes use of this word in the beatitudes: "Blessed are the merciful…" (Matt. 5:7). This word is also used to tell us of the physical sacrifice of Jesus for us. When Timothy reads this word in his letter, he will immediately remember who Jesus Christ is—and the costly grace of Jesus given toward him and for him.

Paul's fourth word for Timothy is the most treasured word in the sacred scriptures, "peace;" *shalom* is the Ancient Hebrew word. Once again, this word here in Paul's sentence, the Greek word ειρηνε (eirene), has its origin in God's decision toward the world. Shepherds heard this word from the nighttime choir on the first

Christmas Eve. "Peace on earth, this is the good decision of God" (Luke 2).

In Paul's conclusion to this greeting, he names God the Father and the Lord Jesus Christ. Some interpreters have wondered why Paul in his greetings does not also name the Holy Spirit. The mystery of the Father, Son, and Holy Spirit is clearly taught in the New Testament gospels, Acts, and the letters. It is clear that the ministry of the Holy Spirit is to point to Jesus Christ and to assure each believer of the living Christ. Our Lord made that clear in the Thursday night discourse, "I will send the one who comes alongside and he will teach you concerning me" (John 14:26). The Holy Spirit confirms Christ's reality in and among the believers, and in doing so the church is created. Karl Barth explained the ministry of the Holy Spirit in a very understandable way when he said, "When I am able to say that the redeeming love and grace that happened at the cross and empty grave is not only a grand reality but that it is *also for me*, that assurance is the ministry of the Holy Spirit in my life."[1]

This means that Paul has said enough when he says, "Grace to you and peace from God the Father and the Lord Jesus Christ." He has spoken of our Trinitarian faith

---

[1]Karl Barth, *Dogmatics in Outline* (New York: Harper & Row, 1959), 137.

in that sentence, because when I trust and believe the grace and peace that is in Jesus Christ, I have experienced the assuring confirmation of the Holy Spirit. When I personally trust Jesus and experience the assurance of his love, I am filled with the Holy Spirit because I can only know Jesus and his grace because of the ministry of the Holy Spirit.

II Timothy 1:3-7 I am grateful to God—whom I worship with a clear conscience, as my ancestors did—when I remember you constantly in my prayers night and day. Recalling your tears, I long to see you so that I may be filled up with joy. I am reminded of your sincere faith, a faith that lived first in your grandmother Lois and your mother Eunice and now, I am sure, lives in you. For this reason I remind you to rekindle the gift of God that is within you through the laying on of my hands; for God did not give us a spirit of cowardice, but rather a spirit of power and of love and of self-discipline.

At the opening of Paul's letters (Galatians is an exception), he always offers a prayer for those who receive his letter. The central themes within the prayers begin with thankfulness to God for the people he addresses. He also makes brief requests of God for those who will read his letter. If we are careful readers of Paul's opening prayers, we are able to sense the apostle's concerns that will later show up in the content of the letter. In Philemon, for example, Paul will directly draw out implications from his prayer for Philemon and his knowledge of Philemon's love for people. He will follow his prayer with the words, "For this reason…." The prayers in the two Corinthian books prepare the Christians at Corinth for the important requests that become major themes in I and II Corinthians. He thanks God in I Corinthians that the Corinthian believers are "not lacking in any spiritual gift." As we know, Paul will then thoughtfully explore the confusion in the Corinthian church concerning that very subject of "spiritual gifts."

As we read II Timothy, we notice Paul's decisive use of the word, "remember." It is as if Paul wants to ensure young Timothy's awareness of his (Timothy's) own history and his unique part in a larger history. We wonder whether this earnest follower of Christ, for whatever reasons, is not as confident of his own valid history as he should be. Perhaps the loss of his biological father has made Timothy unsure of his own root system. We sense Paul's intention by noticing what he "remembers" in his prayer. First, Paul remembers his own ancient fathers and mothers in the history of God's covenant people. Then he tells Timothy that he, Paul, remembers Timothy in prayer constantly day and night. He remembers Timothy's tears of concern and perhaps loneliness, but he quickly adds that in the present—as Paul looks toward the future—he longs to see Timothy, so that Paul may experience the joy of their shared friendship. This line proves to Timothy that he is not only a worker who has carried out important tasks for the Kingdom of God, but he is a present-tense friend.

Paul then relates his own memory of Timothy's sincere faith. He wants the young man to know this, but he also shows his knowledge of Timothy's spiritual root system, in the faith of his mother Eunice and his grandmother Lois. They are believers too, and therefore the young man is not alone as a believer. He has a heritage of faithfulness, even a generation earlier in his faithful grandmother. In this context, Paul tells of hands that have touched Timothy in grace. This reference to commissioning prayer is also a sign of assurance and significance.

This opening prayer in II Timothy is among the most moving and love-filled of any of the opening New Testament prayers. Timothy has been loved into faith, and he has people in his life who are totally sold on him. They have put their hands on him. In my own journey, when I was pastor at First Presbyterian Church of Berkeley, one occasion made a deep impression on me. At a church reception one Sunday, we were honoring the retirement of our church building superintendent, George Kerr and his wife Vera, after his long tenure in the post. The master of ceremonies asked George to share a few words. George was known as a man of very few words, but on that occasion he decided to relate some humorous observations about me. I had spent two summers during my seminary-student days as a youth intern at the church, during which many embarrassing mishaps took place. He told some of those stories, from the summers of 1954 and 1955. I was now back in Berkeley as senior pastor, after eight years in Seattle and six in Manila. George told the stories in his own way, and at the end he made a remark I will never forget. "You know, Earl, Vera and I have prayed for you every day since those two funny summers." I realized then that I had a root system indeed. They had their hands on me, and on who knows how many others too. As Timothy read his letter, he would now know the same thing.

Once more, the word "remember" comes into the prayer. "Timothy, remember to rekindle the gift of God that is within you." Does Paul imply by this sentence that Christian disciples might forget to sustain the fire of the gifts of God in our lives? We know that the answer to that is "yes." It is possible to forget great objective truths, and everyone who has taken an examination in mathematics or history or foreign language syntax knows about that kind of forgetting, in the intellectual spheres of the human brain. But Paul has in mind the forgetfulness of experiences, especially of the gifts of grace and fellowship that have been invested in our character. These highly personal markers of God's faithfulness and goodness need to be rekindled and stirred up, because they need and deserve to be remembered.

After these exhortations to remember, Paul boldly affirms to this young disciple four great facts concerning gifts, one negative followed by three positives. First, God did not give to us a spirit ("wind" is the Greek word) of delirium. This rare Greek word is translated in the NRSV by the odd word choice, "cowardice." The authorized King James translates it as "fear." The root word δειλιας (delias) is also the root of the English "delirious." It is used for the disciples when they were frightened in a storm on Lake Tiberias. The sense of the word is "disorienting fear." That is Paul's intention in using this word, in my view, not "cowardice" or "craven fear" but the more complicated "disorienting fear." He wants Timothy to know this. There are things to be afraid of, and there are fearfully dangerous times that test our courage, but here Paul has in mind the kind of response to danger that is disoriented and confused. He is confident in his young friend. He wants Timothy to keep his head clear and trust in that clear-headedness God has given him.

This very exciting negative is followed by three grand positives that, when fitted together, become gifts from God to help Timothy keep his sanity in the face of the storms of the first-century Roman world, especially during the chaotic time of Emperor Nero.

God gives, then, not the wind of disorienting fear but the wind of:

1. Power — δυναμεως (dunameos) means the energy of strength and durability in the face of stress.

2. Love — αγαπη (agape) is the word here. This word always points our eyes toward the Lord Jesus Christ, who loved us and gave himself for us. This is "word" and "work" united, love that is not a theoretical idea but a concrete event.

3. A healthy mind — σωφρονεω (sophroneo) means a healthy (*sw*) mind (*frone*). The NRSV translates this word "self-discipline," and the authorized King James uses "sound mind." The King James captures the core idea; Paul uses this word in the same way in Romans 12:3, where the NRSV uses the word "sober judgment" and the King James "soberly." In each case, I think "healthy mind" is the most accurate English word choice.

II Timothy 1:8-9a Do not be ashamed, then, of the testimony about our Lord or of me his prisoner, but join with me in suffering for the gospel, relying on the power of God, who saved us and called us with a holy calling, not according to our works but according to his own purpose and grace.

Paul now challenges Timothy in two ways. First, he speaks to Timothy's feelings and interior personal outlook in the face of the imprisonment of his hero, Paul. But there may be an even greater and more important challenge to his feelings; that is, Timothy's anxiety concerning his own role and even his own ability to stay on course as a follower of Christ. Paul uses the "shame" word: "Do not be embarrassed, or blush as one ashamed when you face your own moment to openly give witness to our Lord, nor should you be ashamed of the imprisonment of Paul, the Lord's servant."

Paul then interprets the ways that a man or woman who lived at the midpoint of the first century would understand the political/social environment of 58-68 CE. Imprisonments and persecutions and even public ridicule fit into the norm. Timothy knows this from experience. His hometown is Lystra, and he would remember the frightening stoning incident: Paul could have been killed by an angry mob, except for the fast thinking of Barnabas and the Christians at Lystra. But Timothy also remembers that soon after that violent incident, perhaps only a few days or weeks later, Paul and Barnabas were openly preaching and teaching in that very city. Citizens in Lystra would then hear what Barnabas and Paul had to say, and many would become believers, including the grandmother and mother of Timothy. On a later trip to Lystra, Paul invites this young man to join up with him.

Remembering that history, and the outcome when the story moved forward, is itself a realistic and hopeful antidote to the shame of becoming a victim of rioters, or even a prisoner of official Rome. The shame of embarrassment at such apparent and present public rejection may not be the lasting or final reality. The meaning and hope that one crowd cynically writes off may later be treasured by that same crowd, or an even greater company. Validation of truth may take time. Paul and his Lord have been validated. We who read this book know that.

We are also tempted to be ashamed when what we hold dear is written off, or discounted, by people who seem to matter as thought leaders. The temptation becomes even harsher when these negative voices are pushed forward by the power of a focused fanaticism or a political system. But Jesus is still the Lord, even when the crowd denounces or ignores who he is. As Samuel Johnson once said, "A fly...may sting a stately horse, and make him wince; but [the fly is still a fly, the horse is still a horse]."[2]

Paul follows this interior counsel with a second challenge that is physical and outward. This second sentence sounds like a coach sending a player into a game. Paul does not ignore or understate the real physical danger that Timothy faces. Paul's words are earthy. He uses a strong word, translated in the King James text, "be thou a partaker of the afflictions of the gospel...." The NIV and NRSV translate this sentence, "Join with me in suffering for the gospel." The Greek word κακοπαθεω (kakopatheo) means "hardship," and Paul adds the prefix "with" (συν; sun). Timothy is challenged to physically get into the game, not alone but among all the other players who are on his side. One teammate is Paul. Paul, the "player coach," is sending in a player—a young one, but a tough one. "Timothy, you will get scuffed up in this game but get on the field. It is not that bad when the game is underway. Believe me, I know." That is the sense of Paul's exhortation. I believe the word should be literally understood as "hardship," a better choice than "suffering."

The best part of the challenge to Timothy is within the word "gospel." The hardship Paul describes is aimed

---

[2]This quote has been adapted from: James Boswell, *The Life of Samuel Johnson* (Herts, UK: Wordsworth Editions, 2008), 134.

toward the goal of sharing the good news of God's faith-fulness and love. But Timothy is not in these dangerous places without divine resources. There is hardship for sure, but he is part of a team according to the power of God. The word κατα (kata) could also be translated "by" the power of God or "in" the power of God. Paul then assures Timothy of that power, for God is the one who has made us safe. This plain and clear word "safe" becomes in the New Testament the most personal of all words for redemption. It has within it the warmth of John's word, "wash" (1 John 1:9). Jesus "washes" us to make us clean; it is at the core of our Lord's word "ransom" in Matthew 20: "the son of man came not to be served but to serve and to give his life a *ransom* for many" (Matt. 20:28). It prepares us for the most mysterious word "reconcile" (II Cor. 5), which means to change and create total new-ness. It has the richness of the safety of "peace" in it, and so fulfills the great word of the Old Testament, *shalom*. "Justification" also intends a radical change in a human life. It happens in us as God's righteous character now, as the servant Lord grants forgiveness of our sins and sets us free—"redeems" us from the tyranny of wrongness and guilt. Paul wants Timothy to recognize the immense power within the word "save."

Paul and Timothy, as men saved by the gospel, are the ones who are called (Paul uses the plural) not because they are stronger than others but because of God's purpose and grace. This is the logic of Paul's narrative: God is the one who has saved us, and he is the one who sends us into the contest. His reasons come from his own decision, his purpose and his love.

II Timothy 1:9b-11 This grace was given to us in Christ Jesus before the ages began, but it has now been revealed through the appearing of our Savior Christ Jesus, who abolished death and brought life and immortality to light through the gospel. For this gospel I was appointed a herald and an apostle and a teacher...

This grace already has been given to us in Christ Jesus before time eternal (*chronos aionion*). The NIV translates these words as "before the beginning of time," King James "before the world began," and now it has been manifested through the actual appearance in human history of the Savior Jesus Christ. Paul then describes the power of the good news of Christ as Savior with a remarkable word choice, κατειργασατο (kateirgasato), by which Paul tells Timothy that Jesus has made death inoperative. The root at the core of this word is εργ (erg), which means "work" or "event," as when both Paul and James tell of faith that "works." In this instance, he writes that death is "not working," because the strong negative use of κατα (kata) means "against" or "not."

This requires some explanation. In our Greek text, κατα (kata) is the same logical connective word that appears in chapter 1 verse 1. That text states that the will of God is "for the sake of" the promise. This "for the sake of" is the mild use of the connective Greek word κατα. Later, in chapter 1 verse 8, Paul urges Timothy to join with him in suffering for the gospel "relying on" the power of God, using the same Greek connective word κατα. Then in verse 9, Paul writes that God has called us "not according to" our works but "according to" his own grace and purpose. In this text the Greek for "according to" is again κατα, except that the negative *ou* is used also in one part of the sentence. This makes a tremendous difference. The mild use of κατα means "equal to, because of, in light of." But when κατα is attached to another word, depending on context, it has the reverse sense. Attached as a prefix it usually means "down" or "against," as for example when attached to κρινω (krino), which means to "weigh" or "judge"—but κατακρινω (katakrino) means to "judge down," to "condemn."

When attached to εξουσια (exousia), the word "to rule" (we get the English "executive" from this word), κατεξουσια (katexousia) means "to rule down," as in "tyranny"—also κατακυριευουσιν (katakurieuousin), "to Lord over," "rule down." Attached to στρεφω (strepho), it means "to change, turn, bring up" in a positive sense—but καταστρεφω (katastrepho) means to "tear down," as in II Timothy 2:14 (English "catastrophe" comes from that word).

Here in our text (II Tim. 1:10), κατα attached to εργ (erg) means "not workable." The power of death has become *inoperative.* The NRSV and King James translate the word as "abolished death." The word is also used by Paul in I Corinthians 15:26, where "The last enemy to be destroyed is death." But Paul's point is that death, while it remains a reality within the inner boundary of our life, is not the last word. There is a boundary outside of that inner boundary, and what happened at the cross—by Jesus' actual death—is that death itself has been made non-operative in a profound way, so that Paul can write to the early believers, "O death, where is thy sting." The promise is now fulfilled: "Death is swallowed up in victory" (I Cor. 15:54). Death has lost its power; the light of life has won the victory over corruption, because of the gospel.

The word αφθαρσιαν (aphtharsian) is also used by Paul with the negative *a* as its prefix, and so the English text uses the word "immortality." A greater life is here, against even death and mortality.

Paul then uses three words to describe himself: Because of this new light of life he is a herald (*keryx*, an announcer), an apostle (*apostolos*, one sent like a messenger), and a teacher (*didaskolos*, one who explains the content of the good news.) These three descriptive words become key markers for the purpose of Paul's life.

He sees himself first as an announcer, a witness to what he has seen and heard and personally experienced. This word is a lean word, describing in basic indicative language that the Christian's task is simply to tell what he or she has seen and heard and experienced: "I may not fully understand every implication, but what I have discovered I can honestly report."

The second word is a more directional word. An "apostle" is a messenger sent to represent the interests of the one who sends. It carries within it more intentionality, so that the apostle must use discernment and the skill of wisdom to thoughtfully make sure he or she has rightly represented the sense of the message. The skill of listening is also essential for discernment, so that the apostle rightly understands the questions of those who receive the message. These skills are aimed toward the goal of communication, so that the message is faithfully told and so that it can be heard.

The third word is *didaskolos*, "teach," from which we have the English word "didactic." This tells of a messenger/

herald who seeks to teach the content of a message, so that it is understood without confusion and free from mistakes in content. This third task by its very nature takes more time than the first two, and it takes no less skill. Most of all, the teacher needs to trust the validity and durability of the message itself. This confidence will show up in the teacher's approach to those who are willing to listen and learn. A teacher who teaches subject matter that he or she knows to be true will be able to take the long view toward those who are learning. Such a teacher will not require the aid of deception or the pressure of social influence to establish or persuade the listener. Teaching does require time, but truth is durable. When the morning's slogans of fads and falsehoods have started to fade, truth lasts into the afternoon and evening. C.S. Lewis put it this way: Truth wins out over the long haul; "its hour comes when these wholesale creeds have begun to fail us."[3]

Paul takes this chance with real people in real places, and he encourages Timothy to do so as well.

---

[3]C.S. Lewis, *Miracles* (New York: HarperCollins, 2001), 212.

II Timothy 1:12 ...and for this reason I suffer as I do. But I am not ashamed, for I know the one in whom I have put my trust, and I am sure that he is able to guard until that day what I have entrusted to him.

Paul repeats the words, "I am not ashamed." This phrase is known to us also from Paul's greatest letter, Romans. In Romans 1:16, Paul writes that he is not ashamed of the gospel. In II Timothy 1:8, we hear his encouragement to Timothy: "Do not be ashamed of the witness of the Lord, nor of Paul as his prisoner." Now in 1:12, Paul speaks for himself: "I am not ashamed, because I know whom I have trusted." This use of the "shame" word almost sounds as if it were his commentary on Romans 1:16. In the Romans text, Paul is thankful for the gospel and the power of God who backs up that good news. He boldly uses the word "shame" and then negates it with the strong "no" (ουκ, *ouk*), and therefore with this negative prefix he signals—as he did in the Romans affirmation—its opposite. "I am thankful for the gospel," "I am sold on the gospel," "I am convinced of the gospel," and "I am proud of the gospel."

In II Timothy 1:12, he is gratefully proud and confident because he knows the one in whom he "trusts." Paul then uses the word "persuade" (πειθω, *peitho*), not an absolute word but a word that tells the reader he has enough evidence. It makes clear the fact that he has taken in the evidence, weighed it, and found himself persuaded that the one whom he trusts is a powerful guard for his life. The word for "guard" (φυλαξαι, *phulaxai*) is sometimes translated in the New Testament as "watch over." In Luke 2, we are told that shepherds near Bethlehem on Christmas Eve were "watching over" their sheep. Paul is confident that his Lord is able to "watch" what is entrusted to his care. There is a variation in certain Greek texts that is read in two ways: "able to guard what I have committed to him" or "able to guard what he has committed to me...." Both readings have equally edifying impact for our understanding of the text. Our Lord is able to guard what I have committed to him to that day (NIV, KJV, ASB, NRSV), and "he is able to guard what he committed to me to that day" (RSV). In both instances, my life and my apostleship are in his care. He has the power to watch over me, and he is the trustworthy guard.

This brief sentence of St. Paul is a helpful and realistic statement of the meanings of faith in God. Paul describes the man and woman who have discovered that Jesus—whom we have met in the New Testament narratives and in our own personal journey thus far—is trustworthy and able to keep his promises. Paul makes his wager of faith not so much because of the promises in the law, prophets and writings, or even in the gospel, but because of the one who makes the promises. He tells Timothy, "I know whom I have believed." Paul has tested the trustworthiness of Jesus himself as the keeper of his life, and he tells Timothy that he has enough evidence to keep on trusting. Paul is not using absolute language in this statement of faith, because that would make his affirmation a non-meaning statement—absolutes are impossible for us.[4] Only God is absolute; therefore, our faith is not absolute. We who trust do so on the basis of the evidence we have; therefore because of that evidence, we trust in the faithfulness and love of the one whom we meet in the New Testament accounts.

The mystery of Christian belief in God is that the Holy Spirit assures a believer of the rightness of our trust in Christ, using the inner confirmation that Jesus himself promised (John 14:25, 26). "When we are able to say that God's love and faithfulness is not only truth in a general larger sense but is also for me," that is the assurance of the Holy Spirit. John Calvin explains the ministry of the Holy Spirit this way: "The whole comes to this, that the

---

[4]Blaise Pascal, *Pensees: Thoughts on Religion and Other Subjects,* ed. H.S. Thayer and Elisabeth B. Thayer, trans. William Finlayson Trotter (New York: Washington Square Press, 1965), 22-23.

Holy Spirit is the bond by which Christ effectually binds us to himself."[5] What is important for us to see is that this confirmation does not cancel out our own unique discovery journey, in and with the grace and trustworthiness of Jesus Christ. That discovery is here attested to us by St. Paul, in II Timothy 1:12. Nothing can eliminate his discovery sentence, "I am persuaded." Something has convinced him of the faithfulness and love of Jesus Christ. Paul's affirmation of faith in II Timothy 1:12 becomes for us, as readers of II Timothy, a brief explanation of the dynamics of Paul's own trust in God—of how he came to that faith. For Paul, there are two parts to the act of believing; they focus on his phrases, "I know whom" and "He is able." In both parts, Paul is persuaded because of what he has discovered. His trust is not an irrational or non-rational leap into a mysterious zone of faith. Faith for Paul is an intellectual and moral discovery, just as it is an emotion-filled discovery.

What does he need to know in order to trust in the Savior Jesus Christ? The "whom" is the very center of Paul's faith, and that center is the man Jesus of Nazareth, who is himself the source of the good news. He is the Savior who at the cross saved us and disarmed death itself

---

[5]John Calvin, *Institutes of the Christian Religion* (Grand Rapids, Baker: 1987), Book 3, Chapter 1, Section 1.

on our behalf. In Jesus we discover the powerful event of the Love of God, which has brought the light of life into view. Faith becomes a decision to trust that "event love" that Paul calls the good news.

But Paul himself also needs to wager on the power of God's grace. He must rest his own weight on the foundation of the trustworthiness of Jesus Christ. That putting-down of his weight is the act of believing, either with the turbulence of mixed feelings and questions or with the calm of uncomplicated assurance. Either way, it is a human act to decide to trust in Jesus.

This brief sentence from Paul in II Timothy 1:12 was important in my own story. I came to the University of California, Berkeley as a freshman in 1949. I was a typical secular young man. Although our family had attended church in McCloud, California, I began college without much understanding of Christianity. My first two years were spent focused on weekend hiking, movies, friends, and of course trying to keep up as a student. I do not remember going to church, but in the spring of my sophomore year, a friend—Arba Hudgens—in my co-op dorm (Barrington Hall) invited me to attend a small weekly Bible study group of men. When I met with these fellow students, I was struck by the fact that they were looking at the New Testament letters through young adult eyes.

I was intrigued by this, and when summer came I joined them at a college conference at Lake Tahoe, sponsored by the college group at First Presbyterian Church of Berkeley. Everything was making sense to me, especially a sermon by the pastor of First Presbyterian Church of Berkeley, Rev. Robert Boyd Munger. He put the issue of faith as follows: "When on the basis of what you know about Jesus Christ you are willing to trust in the trust-worthiness of Jesus Christ, then you are ready to become a Christian." I realized then that faith meant putting my weight down on the faithfulness and love of Jesus Christ. Everything else is secondary. In that summer of 1951, I became a believer. I could then say, "I know who I have believed in, and I am persuaded that He is faithful and good and able to keep what I have committed to Him."

II Timothy 1:13,14 Hold to the standard of sound teaching that you have heard from me, in the faith and love that are in Christ Jesus. Guard the good treasure entrusted to you, with the help of the Holy Spirit living in us.

Paul concludes his personal witness to the faithfulness of Jesus Christ as Savior and Messiah with an explanation of the importance of this confidence. He uses two words; he calls the affirmation a "pattern" (υποτυπωσιν, *hupotuposin,* "standard" in NRSV) of "sound teaching"

(NIV, KJV, NRSV). The word "sound" is the word υγι–αινω (hugiaino), which can be translated "healthy." The usual intention of this word υγιη (hugiei) in the New Testament is "healthy," as in John 5:11, "The man who made me well." Paul's point is exactly this: The trust of a believer in the "whom" of our discovery, and in Christ's ability to guard our lives, is the essence of a healthy faith. It would be unhealthy to trust in our own self-mastery through our own strength, or even in the strength of a group of like-minded people who propose to guard the truth and true doctrine. Health at the edges comes from a healthy center. Paul is advocating for a living, growing relationship in Christ as that healthy centeredness.

These are remarkable personal words from the Apostle, concerning his own free decision to trust in Jesus Christ as the trustworthy "whom" of New Testament discipleship. Paul's words are therefore both realistic and healthy. He believed because he saw for himself that the Jesus of the New Testament was both *good* enough to deserve our trust and *strong* enough to fulfill our trust.

Imagine a solo rock climber, who—just as he is nearing the summit of a dangerous ascent—slips on the rock face, just out of the range of a fixed anchor bolt where he needs to snap in a safety carabiner. The climber nevertheless is able to grasp an exposed tree root, which offers at least a temporary rescue. At this point, another climber reaches down from the edge above and grasps both wrists of the climber in peril. "I'll help you get your footing, just let go of the root." We must ask one question in this parable: "What will determine whether the imperiled climber lets go of the root in order to trust the one who offers help toward a better footing?" It all depends on what that climber thinks of the one who offers aid. Imagining myself as the climber in peril, I have to make two decisions. First, I need to assess the good will of my would-be helper. Added to that, I need to assess his strength. In other words, at such a terrifying moment, I have to trust the character of the promiser and his capability to keep the promise. I may not have all the evidence I want, but on the basis of the evidence I do have, I must decide. That deciding moment is what becomes belief in God's character, revealed in the Savior Jesus Christ.

Paul has assured Timothy in verse 12 of very good news, that the Lord of the Gospel Paul teaches guards and continually watches over both pastors, Paul and Timothy. He describes that assurance using the strong word, "healthy teaching" (NRSV "sound teaching"). The saving healthiness of the faithfulness and the love of Christ are at the core of the teaching. Paul challenges Timothy to guard that excellent treasure. This is the same

word "guard," φυλαξ (phulax), that was our assurance
as we experienced the care of the shepherd king who has
watched over our lives and kept us safe. Now we hear
Paul's challenge that we too are mandated to guard the
excellent treasure of the good teaching about Jesus Christ.
Fortunately for us, the Holy Spirit who dwells in us will
enable ordinary disciples to guard this treasure. The question that comes into our minds on hearing this challenge
is this: What are the dangers we must guard against? It
is not Christ who needs our protection, because he is the
living Lord; his love and his truth are not in danger of
loss through the wasting effect of our illness, or even the
character weaknesses of his disciples. No, the good news
of Christ is healthy throughout. What then is the danger?
The danger is that for whatever reasons, we might leave
behind or forget that truth.

Paul will now explain some first-century dangers to
his young friend, and we will read of them as the text of
II Timothy unfolds in front of us. But before certain real
first-century dangers are explained to Timothy, it is useful
to us who read these words in a later time and place to
reflect on these dangers. Paul seeks a higher ground for
safety than any defensive protection that Timothy or we are
able to mount. It is very clear in verses 13 and 14 that the
best defense of the healthy truth of Jesus is for his disciples

to stay healthy themselves, by abiding in the good territory where health is. C.S. Lewis put it this way: "The best safeguard against bad literature is a full experience of good; just as a real and affectionate acquaintance with honest people gives a better protection against rogues than a habitual distrust of everyone."[6]

As a believer in Christ, Paul is not worried in any grave sense about the loss of good news—as long as we stay close to Jesus, who is the reason for and the source of the good news. This essential health of a believer in Jesus is not defensive; nor is it overly suspicious of finding rogues around a corner, though every man or woman must encounter a few rogues during a lifetime. I believe the secret to Paul's unflappable stance of moderation toward the world is found in two simple sentences in another of his prison letters. As Timothy knew, Paul wrote to the Philippians, "Let all people know your moderation, the Lord is alongside of you" (Phil. 4:5). Also his claim, "I can take in stride all things through Him who strengthens me" (Phil. 4:13).

This is a basic healthiness that Paul has already claimed for his young friend Timothy. "God did not give you a spirit of disorienting fear but of power and love and a healthy mind..." (II Tim. 1:7). For Paul, the source of

---

[6]C.S. Lewis, *An Experiment in Criticism* (Cambridge: Cambridge University Press, 1973), 94.

Timothy's health is his relationship with his Savior Lord. This is the best protection of all, free from the toxic effects of defensiveness and fear. Added to that, there is healthy encouragement from a few faithful friends in Christ—and a grandmother and mother, too.

II Timothy 1:15 You are aware that all who are in Asia have turned away from me, including Phygelus and Hermogenes.

Timothy is well acquainted with the Roman province of Asia (modern-day Turkey). He himself is from Lystra, and he now lives at Ephesus. He has been and probably still is involved in ministry in the Ephesian church, where Paul had spent two and half years teaching daily in Tyrannus Hall. Paul tells of two men, Phygelus and Hermogenes, who along with several others have turned away from Paul. They have probably openly challenged the message of the gospel of Christ, which is even more important than a personal break with Paul. Since this is the only New Testament reference to these two, we can only wonder what were their objections to Paul's message. We only know that they were located in the province of Asia. Were they associated with the Galatian crises, in which Jewish believers had insisted that Greeks fulfill the covenant traditions of circumcision and dietary law of the Torah? Or, more likely, were they involved with the early proto-Gnostic teachers that Paul argued against in his Colossian and Ephesian letters? Did the earthly portrait of Jesus in the gospel as fully God and fully man offend them? Did they prefer a more phantom-like Jesus Christ? We know from John's first letter (1 John) that Christians at Ephesus had encountered false teaching that insisted that the Jesus Christ we worship did not come in the flesh, but was pure spirit (1 John 4:1-3). Some of these teachers advocated that the resurrection victory is a mystical/spiritual experience, and that for certain select believers, it has already happened; only those who have the secret "Gnosis" (knowledge) are the winners of this spiritual victory.

Paul opposed both of these false religious/ethical gospels, in his letters to the Galatians and to the Thessalonians (II Thess. 2:1-2). Each of these teachings was unhealthy; each substituted a "hidden truth" discovery, connected to the movement's particular leaders, for the Gospel itself, so that this substitute theory became for them the more "spiritual" message.

A similar false teaching arose in Germany during the 1930s. The so-called German Christian movement insisted on an Aryan "good news" that substituted—in place of biblical Christian faith—a vision of a 1000-year reign of Aryan triumphalism, to be preferred against what Friedrich

Nietzsche had called the "beggarly Jewish religion of the weak savior Jesus of Nazareth." It was hard for Christian believers in the Germany of the 1930s to withstand the mixture of cultural nationalism and its exclusive Aryan racial "good news" theory. Thankfully, at Barmen in 1934, a brave group of Christian laity and pastors dared to stand across the pathway of this anti-biblical distortion. At Barmen was born the Confessing Church Movement within the German Evangelical Church.

Their answer, like St. Paul's, pointed to the true center who is Jesus himself, and to the Old and New Testament witnesses that surround him. Article 1 of the Barmen Declaration puts it this way: "Jesus Christ, as he is attested to us in Holy Scripture, is the one Word of God which we have to hear and which we have to trust and obey in life and in death. We reject the false doctrine…apart from and besides this one Word of God…."

Timothy, who receives this letter while living in Ephesus, now is alerted to two men by name here in 1:15, and to two others later in 2:17. The responsibility for assessing the situation is left in Timothy's hands.

II Timothy 1:16-18 May the Lord grant mercy to the household of Onesiphorus, because he often refreshed me and was not ashamed of my chains; when he arrived in Rome, he eagerly searched for me and found me—may the Lord grant

that he will find mercy from the Lord on that day! And you know very well how much service he rendered in Ephesus.

When we hear the name "Onesiphorus," we have more details to help us understand Paul's reference than we did with Phygelus and Hermogenes. From the later reference in II Timothy 4:19, we realize that Paul's great friends Prisca and Aquila in Ephesus were also friends of the family of Onesiphorus. Here, we learn that this man stood by Paul in spite of the humiliation of imprisonment. Onesiphorus sought him out in Rome, perhaps putting himself in danger.

Friendship is an important ingredient in all of Paul's letters. Paul had a remarkable ability to make friends and to keep them. He stays loyal to his friends, and yet at the same time he alerts Timothy about two unfriendly Ephesian teachers and the group who joined them. I am impressed that the Apostle is not obsessed or preoccupied with the opposition of this group. He simply notes them, almost in a matter-of-fact way. He spends more time focusing on the gift of good friendship from brave Onesiphorus, who went searching in dangerous Rome for one Jewish prisoner from Tarsus.

Paul is realistic in understanding the relationships that are interpersonal as well as ideological. This realism is important, because not every advocacy group will agree with Paul. Nor will every pastor/teacher stay loyal to a man like Paul when pressures mount from other teachers and groups. Theological differences in viewpoint and conviction have an impact on personal relationships between people, just as differences in discipleship strategies and mission goals will often affect interpersonal friendship—as Paul and Barnabas discovered when they disagreed about the role of the younger man, John Mark (Acts 15:36-39). Fortunately for Paul, as he mellowed over the course of his journeys as an apostle, he was reunited in friendship with Mark. The final sentences in II Timothy make this clear.

We welcome that trajectory, as we can trace other breaches of friendship in the fellowship of the band of believers, and we are especially glad when those differences and controversies do not become the final chapter of the story. John Newton was a slave trader early in his young adult years, but not at the end. I am impressed by the fact that many of the discipleship encounters in the gospel records and the book of Acts are unfinished portraits. What we have are partial narratives that need to become parts of a larger narrative. The gospels are decidedly non-propaganda documents, since so many key people and accounts are left in midair, often without happy or fulfilling endings to quote. The narratives in the gospels, the book of Acts and the letters of the New Testament have integrity and truth written all over them. In most of them, the stories are not completed. Stephen, John the Baptist, James the brother of John, and Judas are among the few whose journeys are told to their earthly conclusion. But what about the younger John, or Peter, or Nicodemus? Mary Magdalene, Martha, the rich young ruler, the Pharisee who invited Jesus to dinner, Paul, and even Timothy? We know them midstory, and we must leave the rest of their stories in God's hand. That is even true, in a profounder way, with John the Baptist, Stephen, Judas and others like them. As C.S. Lewis states, "A more Christian attitude…is that of leaving futurity in God's hands. We may as well, for God will certainly retain it whether we leave it to him or not."[7]

II Timothy 2:1-7 You then, my child, be strong in the grace that is in Christ Jesus; and what you have heard from me through many witnesses entrust to faithful people who will be able to teach others as well. Share in suffering like a good soldier of Christ Jesus. No one serving in the army gets entangled in everyday affairs; the soldier's aim is to please the enlisting officer. And in the case of an athlete, no one is crowned without competing according to the rules. It is the farmer who does the work who ought to have the first share of the crops. Think over what I say, for the Lord will give you understanding in all things.

---

[7] C.S. Lewis, *The Weight of Glory* (New York: HarperCollins, 2001), 61.

Paul calls Timothy his "child." He uses the word τεκνον (teknon), which may be translated "child or son." John uses the "little child" diminutive word in 1 John 2:1, τεκνια (teknia), "My little children...." Our Lord uses "little children" on the Thursday night of Holy Week with his disciples: "Little children, I am with you only a little longer..." (John 13:33). Paul sees Timothy almost as a son. Still, he is not addressing him as a "little" son but as a youth, τεκνον, who is becoming a mature leader with a lively, growing mind. Therefore in the text, Paul acknowledges the closeness of his relationship with Timothy yet uses language that emphasizes the decisive strength and decision-making independence Timothy owns as a young man. He describes Timothy as a teacher, who must carefully choose faithful people who will be able to teach others the truth of the gospel of grace. He repeats his earlier encouragement to Timothy, to share in the hardships as a soldier would.

The word "hardships" (NRSV "sufferings") is the same word used in chapter 1 verse 8. Here, Paul draws together three parabolic images of this willingness to engage hardships for the goal of sharing God's grace. He cites the soldier, the athlete, and the farmer. Each must pay the price of the unique hardship and suffering that is the mandate of a soldier, an athlete, or a farmer. Each receives a reward for performing the task and enduring the hardship. At the close of these parabolic examples of discipleship faithfulness, Paul invites his young friend to think over the examples of the soldier, athlete, and farmer in terms of his own present life and discipleship challenges. He promises Timothy that the Lord will be his teacher and will therefore grant him "understanding."

Here, his language choice is "συνεσιν εν πασον" (sunesin en pason). Συνεσις (sunesis) is the Greek word for "intelligence." Paul's promise is expansive and broad: "understanding in everything." The confidence that Paul shows toward Timothy has its own healthy result built in: It frees Timothy to think things through for himself and come to his own conclusions. Paul takes a certain risk, because he must trust in the judgment calls that his ministry partner will make. By this, Paul shows an impressive degree of confidence in Timothy.

When Christian brothers and sisters can offer this kind of trust in honoring the decisions of other Christians, especially in difficult times, the resulting level of interpersonal fellowship in Christ will move deeper. This is particularly the case when issues and/or controversies exist, causing earnest Christians in one place and context to hold to different interpretations and opinions from other, equally earnest Christian brothers or sisters who live in another place and context.

During the height of the Cold War, I saw this profound solidarity of respect and understanding expressed in the lives of two great Christian statesmen, Joseph Hromadka and John A. Mackay. Mackay was President of Princeton Theological Seminary, 1936-1959. His longstanding friend, the theologian Joseph Hromadka, had been for a time a scholar/teacher at Princeton but had decided to stay in Prague following the Soviet takeover of Czechoslovakia. Hromadka was accused of being procommunist by many in Western Europe and in the USA because of his apparent approval of the Czechoslovakian government. John Mackay said to his friend, "Joseph, I don't fully understand your decisions but I trust you." I was present during the World Council of Churches meeting in Uppsala, Sweden, in 1968, at a Princeton Alumni luncheon. There, Hromadka paid tribute to Dr. Mackay and expressed how much his friend's trust meant to him during those hard years—hard for himself and for the Christian Church in Eastern Europe. He was trusted as a fellow believer in Jesus Christ, and Paul offers the same assurance of solidarity and trust in his words assuring Timothy: "For the Lord will give you understanding in all things" (2:7).

I believe that Paul's discipleship/spiritual leadership pattern in this relationship with Timothy is instructive for all who serve at posts of leadership and leadership training.

Paul's goal is not a rigid compliance, nor is it a chain-of-command model of leadership. His goal is to encourage this young teacher to examine the grand center of Christian faith—the person of Jesus himself—and then as a disciple of Jesus to carefully study the Holy Scriptures, where he sees the good news in action. The three parabolic images of the soldier, athlete, and farmer help Timothy to weigh and interpret the meanings of the whole gospel in the particular setting of his own life challenges. Paul trusts in the Holy Spirit's abiding influence in the life of his colleague in ministry. The result is a leader who is better able to think for himself, to make real decisions many miles from the physical presence of his teacher/mentor Paul.

II Timothy 2:8-10 Remember Jesus Christ, raised from the dead, a descendant of David—that is my gospel, for which I suffer hardship, even to the point of being chained like a criminal. But the word of God is not chained. Therefore I endure everything for the sake of the elect, so that they may also obtain the salvation that is in Christ Jesus, with eternal glory.

"Remember Jesus Christ, raised from the dead, a descendant of David's seed." "Remember" is a vital word in the vocabulary of faith, both in the Old Testament and in the New Testament.

Psalm 77 is a lament Psalm, in which the anguished writer wonders if God has forgotten to love because of his anger against his people. But midway into the Psalm, the writer decides to remember the goodness of God toward his people, which God proved when he brought Israel out of the bondage of Egypt. "I will remember your wonders of old..." (77:11). The Psalmist remembers the concrete acts of God: "with your strong arm you redeemed your people..." (77:15). "Remember" is also a key word in Psalm 119:93, Psalm 103:2, and Isaiah 40:21.

Paul points to the greatest memory of all, the historical fact that the person Jesus has defeated death. He is the one we remember. This Jesus is the fulfillment of all that the great Jewish King David signifies, not only spiritually but concretely, since he is David's seed. Jesus as the descendant of David has completed David's legacy. Jesus is the only one able to resolve David's tragedy and treachery, and he fully embodies David's greatness. Therefore this Jesus is the Messiah. He stands at history's center not as a symbol but as the concrete, real man, Jesus of Nazareth—the man of the cross on Good Friday and the empty tomb on Easter.

The concreteness of this sentence as Paul wrote it was impressive to the church fathers, who especially noted the actuality of our Lord's death and victory. John Chrysostom asks, "Why is this mentioned? It is directed chiefly against the heretics... for upon this point many had already begun to subvert God's providence, being ashamed at the immensity of God's love for humanity."[8] Christ's love is both physical and spiritual. It is total help for total need.[9]

Paul then repeats an earlier sentence. Because of this good news, Paul is now in chains at Rome. But he follows that fact with a great affirmation: "But the word of God is not chained." The hardworking disciple Timothy deserves to remember this too. As an athlete, soldier, and farmer he needs to know the larger facts beyond the particular battle in his particular place—or at the athletes' training camp, where everyone is exhausted by repetitious laps of conditioning runs—or in the apparently nonproductive plowing of soil, with (for now) no crops to show for it. He needs to know that the living words of truth, love, hope, and life cannot be chained for long, though the chains indeed have present oppressiveness that cannot be ignored. The chains' power is like darkness, but it is a darkness that only has temporary authority. Light, even faint light, is stronger than darkness. Paul has decided to

[8]John Chrysostom, "Homilies on II Timothy" in *Colossians, 1-2 Thessalonians, 1-2 Timothy, Titus, Philemon,* vol. 9 of *Ancient Christian Commentary on Scripture: New Testament,* ed. Peter Gorday (Downers Grove, IL: InterVarsity Press, 2000), 243.
[9]Barth, *Dogmatics,* 107.

put his weight down on the power of God's decision ("word") that cannot be finally chained. He has said this in his letter to the Romans: "Neither death, nor life, nor angels, nor rulers, nor things present... nor anything in all creation will be able to separate us from the decision God made when he loved in Jesus Christ our Lord" (Romans 8:38).

The Christians who met at Barmen, Germany in 1934 decided to preface their final affirmation of the Declaration (Article 6) with these words, first from Jesus: "Lo I am with you always, to the close of the age" (Matt. 28:20). And then from Paul: "The word of God is not fettered" (II Tim. 2:9). The salvation in Jesus Christ is indeed, as John Chrysostom described it, the event that shows "the immensity of God's love for humanity."[10]

II Timothy 2:11-13 The saying is sure:

If we have died with him, we will also live with him;
if we endure, we will also reign with him;
if we deny him, he will also deny us;
if we are faithless, he remains faithful—
for he cannot deny himself.

Paul now quotes what he describes as a "faithful saying." We cannot find a source for this saying in any

---

[10]Chrysostom, "Homilies on II Timothy," 243.

89

other Old or New Testament book. Therefore, it may be a discipleship hymn that perhaps Christians in Ephesus would have known. Paul describes the saying as "faithful" (πιστις, *pistis*). This quotation is in a poetic form and preserves a parallelism balance in the first three strophes. "If we died in him, we will live with him." This first strophe is a sentence of consolation and encouragement for those who are facing the real dangers of deadly persecution.

The second strophe is also a sentence of encouragement, for the believers to maintain faithful loyalty when confronted by dangers. "If we endure [υπομενω, *hupomeno*, is the word for 'endurance, steadfastness'], we will reign with him." This line does not overstate the bravery and courage of the believers, as if they were superheroes. Instead it makes use of the endurance word upomenw, "staying under, hanging on, enduring." But the promise is larger than we would expect. For endurance, the reward is not merely survival at the end of the day but a role in governance along with the Lord of the hymn. We will reign with him.

The third strophe is a heavy equation, which the parallelism in the poem would seem to require. "If we deny him, he will deny us." This is a somber consequence, and we cannot describe this strophe as encouraging. This saying describes a loss of faith in a time of stress, perhaps because of fear or extremity. Peter lost his faithfulness during surprise challenges, in the middle of the night on the Thursday of Holy Week, so that he denied the Lord at a moment of testing. If and when that happens, the hymn tells us that we deserve the Lord's denial of us. The saying puts that expectation in front of us without equivocation.

But in the fourth strophe, we discover a surprise that breaks the logical order of the saying as a poem. Each of the first three strophes concludes with a consequence for the people of the saying. Line 1—We will live because of Christ; Line 2—We will reign with Christ; Line 3—Christ will deny us, as a consequence of our own denial. Now in strophe four, there is a surprise interpretation and interruption of the logic of the poem.

"If we are against-faithfulness [απιστος, *apistos*] ..." In Greek usage, the a signals "against," "not," or "away from" when it initiates a noun, as in *atheos*—atheist, "against God," or *agnosis*—agnostic, "against knowing." In the fourth strophe, we expect that Jesus will be "against" in faithfulness to match our απιστος, our non-faith; but the poem does not describe that consequence for us. Christ does not become απιστος. Instead, the fourth line says that he is faithful in the face of our failure, in spite of our faithlessness, in the midst of our faithlessness.

The NRSV text of verses 11-13 concludes with the word "faithful," and that word is then followed textually by a linguistic dash mark, which shows that the NRSV translators conclude textually that the poem ends after the first three couplets. Therefore, the next words are not a part of the poem. They are the words of Paul, his commentary on the final line of the poem: "For he cannot deny himself."

This is the good news surprise. The hymn turns our attention away from ourselves and toward Christ. Paul wants to make sure Timothy knows this surprise, which turns our attention back to the grand promise of the hymn, which is—*who* is—the Lord of the song. We may be weak or even cowardly, as was Peter on the night of our Lord's trial. Because of our weakness and failure, like his, we too can expect Jesus to deny us when we deny him. But we know from the history of Holy Week, and the events that happened after Jesus' resurrection, that Peter's denial in the courtyard of the High Priest's palace was not answered by a denial from Jesus. Jesus saw Peter that night, and Peter went out into the night to weep bitterly, but Jesus later found Peter at the Lake of Galilee. Jesus put into place a new equation that neither Peter nor we have any right to expect. At the lake, Jesus does not ask Peter, "*Did* you love me?" Instead he asks Peter, "*Do* you love me?" Even on Easter morning, the women who have just seen the empty tomb are told by the angel, "He is not here; go and tell the disciples and Peter." This new equation alters the third strophe of the saying in a radically new and permanent way. Jesus is faithful, and at the heart of his faithfulness is the salvation of sinners who are healed by grace, even of the moral, spiritual, and character failure of human denial. This is the best news of all.

II Timothy 2:14-19 Remind them of this, and warn them before God that they are to avoid wrangling over words, which does no good but only ruins those who are listening. Do your best to present yourself to God as one approved by him, a worker who has no need to be ashamed, rightly explaining the word of truth. Avoid profane chatter, for it will lead people into more and more impiety, and their talk will spread like gangrene. Among them are Hymenaeus and Philetus, who have swerved from the truth by claiming that the resurrection has already taken place. They are upsetting the faith of some. But God's firm foundation stands, bearing this inscription: "The Lord knows those who are his," and, "Let everyone who calls on the name of the Lord turn away from wickedness."

There are two questions on our minds when we read this next sentence, "Remind them of this." Remind them of what? And remind who of it? I believe the context of the sentence and its grammatical force point to the final line that Paul added to the saying quoted above. Paul is saying, "Remind those who are troubled by the saying—especially by its discouraging third line, that tells those who deny the Lord what they can rightly expect—remind them of the faithfulness of Jesus Christ." Paul contrasts the faithfulness of Jesus with the judgmental consequences of the third strophe, addressing those who read its judgment as a weight that we know is now upon us. The second "deny"—his potential denial of us—in return for the first "deny"—our potential denial of him—makes sense, except that the Savior himself stands as mediator between the judgment and the judged. And, as the fourth strophe reminds us, this one who stands between is the one who is faithful. He is the Lord who does not deny himself. He is the one who makes all the difference. Our faith reaches out to this very Lord in trust, just as Peter did at the Lake of Galilee. Our faith, like Peter's, is answered by the faithfulness and grace of the Lord.

Then comes a warning from Paul: Avoid wrangling over words, which does not benefit the people in the argument. Μαχη (mache) is the word for "fight" or "battle," and λογος (logos) is the word for "word." Paul combines the two words, so that his literal meaning is a warning against a "fight over words." Paul tells Timothy that "word battles" are not useful. Χρησιμον (chresimon) means "beneficial," as in Matthew 20:28, where Jesus says of himself that he came to "benefit humanity and give his life as ransom for many."

By contrast, the war over words, including the words of this saying, is not beneficial. According to Paul, it will "undermine" (καταστροφη, *katastrophe*, "throw down;" we get the English word "catastrophe" from this word) those who engage in such wrangling. Those who hear such verbal warfare are not benefitted either, but harmed. This becomes clear from his immediate naming of two other false teachers who perhaps live at Ephesus, Hymenaeus and Philetus. They and their circle are teaching that a special spiritual resurrection of believers has already taken place, and therefore those who lack the special "gnosis" mystery have been left behind. This Gnostic teaching created a spiritualized interpretation of who Jesus Christ is, as a phantom-like pure spirit. Therefore, what would constitute salvation for us becomes an escapist triumph beyond the physical; it becomes a mystic advance into the realm of greater gnosis. These false teachers have swerved away from the truth about Jesus and his concrete, actual salvation of believers. They have moved into territory that Paul warns will destroy, like the deadly and destructive infection of gangrene; in fact, Paul's actual word choice is the Greek word for "gangrene."

Paul's answer to that false victory message points to the foundation that is permanent and solid, upon which we should build our faith. He assures Timothy that truth bears an inscription, "The Lord knows who are his." We might as well leave our lives in God's hands and trust his promise that his sheep know him and he knows his sheep. We are reminded of Jesus' words in John 10, "Neither shall anyone pluck them out of my hand." This assurance is good enough for Paul, and he offers no other proof to stand against the esoteric false teachings of Hymenaeus and Philetus. These two names have no other citation evidence in the New Testament, but Timothy may know them from his own encounters with them and the circle they occupy. Paul will instead give attention to the positive themes of the good news of Jesus Christ, showing Timothy that he too should give himself to that good news truth and trust in its healing validation.

II Timothy 2:20-26 In a large house there are utensils not only of gold and silver but also of wood and clay, some for special use, some for ordinary. All who cleanse themselves of the things I have mentioned will become special utensils, dedicated and useful to the owner of the house, ready for every good work. Shun youthful passions and pursue righteousness, faith, love, and peace, along with those who call on the Lord from a pure heart. Have nothing to do with

stupid and senseless controversies; you know that they breed quarrels. And the Lord's servant must not be quarrelsome but kindly to everyone, an apt teacher, patient, correcting opponents with gentleness. God may perhaps grant that they will repent and come to know the truth, and that they may escape from the snare of the devil, having been held captive by him to do his will.

Paul creates for Timothy, the young pastor and teacher, a parable of a large house. The analogy is designed to encourage Timothy's character development, but Paul also has a larger strategic purpose in mind.

Paul itemizes different kinds of household utensils that make up the dynamic mission of the "good work" of the house. Each utensil is uniquely shaped for its intended use, and the materials of which they are made are also noted. Each utensil has tasks, some of which are ordinary and some of which are special. In Paul's parable, no further explanation is offered to distinguish what is "ordinary use" and what is "special use;" that decision is left in the hands of the owner of the house. Instead, Paul focuses on the responsibilities of the disciples, which are symbolized by the various grades of the utensils in the analogy. Their task, in the terms of the parable, is simply to wash themselves so that they are ready and prepared for every good work, whatever the owner of the great house has in mind.

Clearly, here Paul is focused on the strategic ministry challenges of his young colleague Timothy. Because of that purpose, he urges Timothy not to give in to the "youthful desires" that as a young leader he would experience. Particularity is signaled by the words Paul chooses: επιθυμιας (epithumias) "strong desire," and νεωτερικας (neoterikas) "common to youth." This suggests a question: What are the unique, desire-related temptations that would most endanger a young pastor like Timothy in his particular time and setting?

I believe the answer is clarified in the two sentences that follow. First, he urges Timothy to commit himself to the largest themes of Christian discipleship: "Pursue righteousness, faith, love, peace so that you may call on the Lord with a clean heart"—καθαρας καρδιας (katharas kardias) "a heart washed clean." "Heart" in the New Testament often refers to the motivational core of the human conscience. These large themes of faith and hope and peace, if embraced by Timothy with the motivation of a washed conscience, will make the next sentence possible for a highly spirited and brave young man: "Have nothing to do with stupid and senseless controversies, you know about them; you know that they breed quarrels." The word translated "quarrel" is again a war word, μαχας (machas), which is one of the New Testament words for "battle." As a verb, it is the word "fight." Youth are more easily tempted than older adults toward violence and μαχας, perhaps because of their eagerness for immediate personal action when challenged. We remember the tense scene in John 8, when a crowd was tempted to stone a woman. John tells us that Jesus said, "Let him without sin cast the first stone." The crowd left "from the oldest to the youngest." The personal desire for immediate, even physical action that was evident in that scene may in fact be the "youthful desire" or runaway zeal that Paul is here seeking to moderate in the young pastor/strategist Timothy. Paul is calling for a calming confidence in the faithfulness of God when confronted by real dangers, and even beyond that a confidence in the power of truth to make its own mark and win over, given time, even the ones who now oppose the way of truth. Paul offers as his strategy the role of the teacher who teaches through and within the territory of error and in that way challenges false and destructive ways. Paul describes the teacher who teaches with kindness and meekness; the word "meek" used in verse 24 is the same word used by Jesus in the third beatitude, "Blessed are the meek [the teachable ones], for they will inherit the earth."

Following Paul's strategy will take time, but it is an approach that trusts in the validity of God's truth to finally make sense to persons who are now entrapped by false assumptions and certitudes, so that "perhaps" (Paul uses this modest word) they will respect and come thereby into the healthy and good place of knowing truth, where they will be freed from the snare of the evil one, the devil. Paul and Barnabas made this teaching strategy their answer to the violent stoning attack on Paul at Lystra, as narrated by Luke in Acts 14. Within days after that brutal outburst, they were back in Lystra teaching the good news. On this visit people listened, and many became believers. One who did was a teenager named Timothy.

This is the moderate and thoughtful strategy that Paul advises in the face of the false teaching of Hymenaeus and Philetus and their cultic followers. Paul urges Timothy not to panic with disorienting fear, but to use his head, take his time, and teach the truth when and where he can, leaving the convincing to the power and love of the Holy Spirit of God.

II Timothy 3:1-9 You must understand this, that in the last days distressing times will come. For people will be lovers of themselves, lovers of money, boasters, arrogant, abusive, disobedient to their parents, ungrateful, unholy, inhuman, implacable, slanderers, profligates, brutes, haters of good, treacherous, reckless, swollen with conceit, lovers of pleasure rather than lovers of God, holding to the outward form of

godliness but denying its power. Avoid them! For among them are those who make their way into households and captivate silly women, overwhelmed by their sins and swayed by all kinds of desires, who are always being instructed and can never arrive at a knowledge of the truth. As Jannes and Jambres opposed Moses, so these people, of corrupt mind and counterfeit faith, also oppose the truth. But they will not make much progress, because, as in the case of those two men, their folly will become plain to everyone.

The third chapter begins with a graphic description of the spiritual and moral stresses that describe the midpoint of the first century. Paul lists bad human decisions that confront Timothy as a servant of the Lord Jesus Christ. Paul uses the phrase "in the last days" as a locating description. The Greek word "last" (εσχατον, *eschaton*) is also used by John in I John 2:18. In the same way, John tells his readers, "Children, this is the last hour...." He does not mean that no more days will happen, or that no more time remains on the clock, but that we are nearer the last boundary of time than we were before. This prophetic shortening of time is a mark of each of the New Testament writers. James uses eschaton in the same way in James 5:3. The prophet Joel's Old Testament use of the phrase is quoted by Peter in his Pentecost sermon, Acts 2:17. Paul does not refer to the stresses as if he is surprised that they exist. In this time of eschaton, he begins the list with an alert to Timothy that he should know and expect such dangers.

But there is good news, and that is that the final "last" belongs to the Lord of every time boundary. We may do harm, but not ultimate harm. Karl Barth explains this eschaton boundary, which belongs to God, by saying that our mischief is real but we cannot do "ultimate mischief." It is noteworthy that each of the grim and hurtful dangers that will now appear on the list is the result of bad "freedom decisions" made by the human players in the human story. The evil one, the devil, tempts—but we decide. The snare of the devil in chapter 2 verse 26 is the tempting power of evil, but our decisions enable that entrapment.

The list starts with the arrogance of the love of self, φιλαυτοι (philautoi). The word combines φιλεω (phileo), one of the traditional love words in the Greek language, and αυτο (auto), self. Each of Paul's word choices shows a free choice on our part, by which we can choose against trust and loyalty to God in favor of our own self-focused ethics and spirituality. It all begins with this first entrapment, the deception that says we deserve to be at the center. That is the snare that opens up the way of selfishness and moral discontinuity, in which I sever my will from loyalty to God, loyalty to God's law, and loyalty to the belovedness of my neighbor in God's sight. All this severs my life from the true source of belovedness—from God. Dietrich Bonhoeffer describes this as counterfeit grace, "a form of godliness, but having denied the power thereof;"[11] "cheap grace is the grace we bestow on ourselves."[12]

Paul makes a historical reference to two sorcerers who tempted Moses with magic arts before Pharaoh. In the Exodus 7:11 narrative, the magicians are not named. Paul quotes their names from Jewish tradition in later Targum writings, not from the Exodus 7 text. Paul's key point is that their deception did not win out at the end of the day, or even partway to the end. Evil acts are disrupted and finally fall apart from the essential flaws that are in the very design of self-arrogance. On that note, Paul concludes this part of his description of the moral and spiritual mischief that his century, as well as ours, must encounter.

II Timothy 3:10-13 Now you have observed my teaching, my conduct, my aim in life, my faith, my patience, my love, my steadfastness, my persecutions, and my suffering the things that happened to me in Antioch, Iconium, and Lystra. What

---

[11]Dietrich Bonhoeffer, *Cost of Discipleship* (New York: Touchstone, 1995), 77.
[12]Ibid., 44.

persecutions I endured! Yet the Lord rescued me from all of them. Indeed, all who want to live a godly life in Christ Jesus will be persecuted. But wicked people and impostors will go from bad to worse, deceiving others and being deceived.

Paul writes autobiographically about his experiences as a messenger of the gospel. What he will now narrate is not new or different information for Timothy, which Paul makes clear in his opening sentence, "You have followed along with me." He uses the word "to follow" here, which the American Standard Bible preserves for us. The NIV renders the text "you know all about," but the word in the Greek text is "follow" παρακολουθεω (parakoloutheo), not "know" γινωσκω (ginosko). The whole atmosphere of the sentence is better understood using the term "follow." Timothy knows about Paul's life experiences, and about his character markers, from actual interpersonal companionship with Paul—as well as reports from other people. It is clear from the text that Paul has told him personally about incidents in his life and ministry that predate his travels with Timothy.

The sense of the text is therefore, "You have followed along with me enough that you know personally about my teaching and my way of living." The word for "way of living," αγωγη (agoge), is from the root verb αγω (ago), which means "to lead, to bring with." Timothy has experienced the teaching of the apostle and the way of living that have marked Paul's life choices. His list continues: "My purpose, my faith, my patience, my love, my endurance, my persecutions, my sufferings...."

The word "persecution" is the severe word διωγμοις (diogmois), a verb that literally means to "run down upon." The word would be used in ordinary first-century Greek to describe chariot races in the arena, in which charioteers would run down to the death helpless people on foot. Paul uses this graphic word three times in this autobiographical paragraph, in 3:11 and 3:12. (The word also was chosen by Paul in a positive sense in II Timothy 2:22, where he challenges Timothy in his own character development to hunt down and pursue righteousness, faith, love, and peace.) At this point, Paul tells of actual places where the harshest meaning of this verb—to "hunt down, run down"—had been Paul's experience; he mentions Antioch, Iconium, and Lystra. These cities are all in a geographical area that Timothy knows very well, especially his own city, Lystra. But the good news is that Paul survived each of these dangerous times in his life. God rescued him. In his second letter to the Corinthians, he tells in a similar way of his experiences in which God enabled him to survive against heavy odds: "We are afflicted in every way, but not crushed, perplexed but not despairing; persecuted but not forsaken" (II Cor. 4:8).

It is clear, in this narrative of the dangers that Jesus' followers faced in the time of Paul's writing, that hardships go with ministry and mission. Dangers are a part of the journey, but a greater and more lasting power is at work in their favor, far greater than the power that is against them.

Though this protection of the Lord is real, nevertheless the reality of persecution will not go away. Paul follows this realistic prediction by explaining how the dangers will possibly continue to unfold. "Evil people and imposters will advance...." The word translated "imposter" is γοητος (goetos), "swindler," and the word for "evil" is πονηρος (poneros). That word *poneros*, when used in its physical sense, means grave sickness, in which the body is bent away from health. In its moral sense, it is the most commonly used New Testament word for evil and wickedness. A parallel word is πορνεια, *porneia*, which is the twisted evil of unhealthy and unlawful sexual relationship—from which we have the English words "pornographic" and "pornography." Paul alerts Timothy that he should not be surprised to find these kinds of moral and spiritual confusion among first-century peoples, even as those who practice such behaviors move on from "bad to worse deceiving and being deceived."

The word translated "deceive" is πλαναω, *planao*. This word is used in 1 John 1:8: "If we say we have no sin we are deceiving ourselves." It is used in Revelation 2:20, in describing a false teacher as "Jezebel," who "calls herself a prophet and is teaching and deceiving my servants." What is interesting about this word is that its root meaning as a noun is "adrift, roaming, wandering." Therefore as a verb, it means "to lead astray." In ancient Greek astronomy, even before Copernicus, astronomers were suspicious of the "stars" that did not twinkle like the North Star. Therefore, this word was used to describe the objects that seemed to be adrift in the skies—like Venus, Mars, and Jupiter. Therefore they are called "planets." They are "deceiving, wandering" stars, and therefore a sea captain should not set his course by them. He should use the North Star, or if below the equator the Southern Cross, to navigate—but not Venus.

This word *planao* becomes a major New Testament word for the temptation to error. Wanderlust has never been a good guide for finding the right pathway for ethical decisions, whether for life goals or for everyday living. In Mark Twain's classic story Huckleberry Finn, the boy Huck, adrift on the Mississippi River, is carried by the current of the river. His story would show only the adriftness of a runaway boy on a raft, except for his wiser companion Jim. Adriftness by itself is interesting, because of the river and its story, but for a man or a boy to set a wise course, there needs to be more than adriftness.

II Timothy 3:14-17 But as for you, continue in what you have learned and firmly believed, knowing from whom you learned it, and how from childhood you have known the sacred writings that are able to instruct you for salvation through faith in Christ Jesus. All scripture is inspired by God and is useful for teaching, for reproof, for correction, and for training in righteousness, so that everyone who belongs to God may be proficient, equipped for every good work.

Paul now points Timothy to the North Star. "But as for you, abide and live in what you have learned and what has rightly won your respect." Paul uses the word abide (μενε, *mene*)— that is the same word our Lord uses in the Thursday night discourse with his disciples, "Abide in me, and my words abide in you" (John 15:7). This relationship word is followed by a knowledge word, μανθανω (manthano). It means to learn from experience, or from someone as from a teacher. Paul uses this word in Philippians 4:9 and 4:11: "What I have learned en route." This knowing word is followed by the word πιστεως (pisteos), from which we have the English word "epistemology," the testing of textual material to know its real meaning. Paul is saying that as Timothy has lived in the texts of the sacred writings, he has learned from them and has found them trustworthy. Paul makes use of the word "holy," *hieros* (Sometimes spelled *jieros*; this word is added to the Hebrew *shalom* [peace] to form the city name *Jerusalem*). The word "holy" is used also to identify the writings we know as the Old Testament. These Holy Scriptures are empowered, and Paul uses the word "empowered," δυναμενα (dunamena). The NRSV translates this as "able"—the scriptures are "able" to make Timothy wise for discipleship training and for ordinary living, just as much as the ministry and leadership challenges that lie before him.

II Timothy 4:1-2 In the presence of God and of Christ Jesus, who is to judge the living and the dead, and in view of his appearing and his kingdom, I solemnly urge you: proclaim the message; be persistent whether the time is favorable or unfavorable; convince, rebuke, and encourage, with the utmost patience in teaching.

Paul here makes use of the strong "presence" word ενωπιον (enopion), which literally means "in front of." The word is used by our Lord in the parables of Luke 15 about the lost sheep, lost coins, and lost sons, with the wonderful line, "I tell you, there is joy in the presence of [in front of] the angels of God over one sinner who repents." This active word now is used to describe Timothy and Paul's encounter "in front of" the Lord, who is the judge of all things and who has brought his kingdom into view. It is in this place where Timothy receives his solemn mandate. The question for Timothy and for each of us who read this letter is this: What is that mandate for Timothy? Is it still the mandate for the Christian disciple today?

The first sentence in the mandate is direct, but with very wide implications: "preach the word." Our theological word *kerigma* comes from this verb, κηρυξον (keryxon), "to announce openly." The NRSV makes use of the English word "message" as the object of the sentence, but I prefer the more basic translation "word." In the text, the simple word *logos* is used. We know from the sentences in chapter 3 that Paul is referring by this mandate to the texts of the sacred scriptures, which point to the living center, who is Jesus Christ. The Old Testament in anticipation always leads us toward the Messiah, who is the fulfillment of the law and prophets and songs of the ancient texts. We who now live in the presence of that fulfillment see that the New Testament gospels and letters also faithfully point us toward the same living center, Jesus Christ. The Old Testament in anticipation and the

New Testament in witness surround Jesus. I believe John Calvin is right in saying that the authority of the written Bible comes from its living center, to which the written words point. The written words derive their authority from the one who is the fulfillment of the texts.

Paul's next word to Timothy is "prepared" (NIV), "ready" (NASB), or "persistent" (NRSV). Greek επιστηθι (epistethi) has the sense of "sudden, immediate, ready for whatever might come." Paul means that Timothy needs to be ready when the time is favorable and when time is not favorable. NIV translates ευκαιρως (eukairos) as "in season," NRSV as "time is favorable."

The second word is ακαιρως (akairos), NIV "out of season" and NRSV "time is unfavorable." In the Greek language, the prefix ευ means "good"—as in ευλογος (eulogos)—"good word," hence "eulogy." ευφωνη (euphone)—"good sound," hence "euphemism." Here the word καιρος (kairos) is used, which means "time in its larger sense," such as "season." This is unlike *chronos*, the Greek word for hours and minutes and seconds (hence the English "chronology"). Paul's challenge to Timothy is plain. "Be ready, Timothy, if the season is good—and in the same way be ready when the season is not good. Your task is to be ready for each, without panic or confusion either way."

The mandate then follows with three strategy words: challenge, warn, and encourage. ελεγξον (elenxon) (NIV "correct," NRSV "convince," NASB "reprove") means "to expose or lay bare," as in John 3:20 "...all who do evil hate the light... so that their deeds may not be exposed." It is therefore a truth-seeking word. The second strategy word is επιτιμησον (epitimeson), "to warn, rebuke" (NIV, NASB, and NRSV all have "rebuke"). As in Luke 17:3, "If another disciple sins you must rebuke the offender," this means to care enough to challenge the wrong when you see it. The third strategy word is παρακαλεσον (parakaleson). This means "to encourage, come alongside" (NIV "encourage," NASB "exhort," NRSV "encourage").

Paul surrounds all three mandate words with his counsel to "patiently" teach all three. This word, μακροθυμια (makrothymia), we heard from Paul earlier in the letter. Now he repeats it again. Then he adds the adverb παση (pase), which means "all, every, in all respects." The NIV and NASB note this using the English translation "with great patience," NRSV "with the utmost patience."

Paul says that even in awkward seasons, Timothy needs to take the long view in his relationships with the people he meets. The counsel stays the same in good seasons, too. Timothy is to teach the truth and to trust that the good news will validate itself over the long journey.

Timothy needs to patiently remember that in each mid-story encounter, the story is not over. Once again, his confidence will be that the Lord of the great story will prove his love, faithfulness and truth to each one, even if they only know and care about the immediate chapter that is now underway in their journey.

Paul has discovered that when a teacher is committed to truth, and to integrity of method in teaching truth, then that teacher can take the long view, patiently teaching through an unfavorable time—knowing that even in such unfavorable hours or days, wrong choices will run up against the very stationary goads that Paul had himself run up against, during his own religiously arrogant time of life and method. Evil, large or small, has within it the seeds of its own "fall apart" or collapse. The teacher should not be surprised at the apparent successes of wrongness, but should stay the course with truth—wisely, with confidence in the greater strength of goodness. Sooner or later, openness to the power of God's grace and faithfulness will show up. When that happens, or even when it begins to happen, the hard shell of cynicism and fanatical zealotry will begin to show cracks. When that moment comes, the teacher needs to be there. It is in the tentative moments of beginning openness that the gospel Paul taught and lived begins to make sense. It wins to grace a Roman guard, a self-focused and lonely man or woman—or a deeply harmed and wounded one—or a young and free-spirited teenager who is caught by surprise in a breakthrough of holy truth that he or she had thought wasn't needed. Somehow, a preparation has happened. God makes it possible for someone who is in mid-story to see, if only in part, the big story—and who it is that has loved us the whole way.

II Timothy 4:3-5 For the time is coming when people will not put up with sound doctrine, but having itching ears, they will accumulate for themselves teachers to suit their own desires, and will turn away from listening to the truth and wander away to myths. As for you, always be sober, endure suffering, do the work of an evangelist, carry out your ministry fully.

Paul is a wise and strategically hopeful interpreter of the hope of the good news of Jesus Christ—not only because of the depth of his faith, but also because he is realistic about the intellectual atmosphere of his century. At this point in his memo about Timothy's strategy as an interpreter of the gospel, Paul discusses the ideological preferences of the first-century audience to which Timothy is an ambassador of truth.

Paul lists several of their preferences: First, people will distance themselves from healthy teaching. Paul uses the same word for health that he used earlier in the letter (II Tim. 1:13), when he described the "wholeness" of the message about the faithfulness and love of Jesus Christ. He states this description forcefully, but now regretfully, as a wholeness that many will want to avoid. They will not tolerate healthy teaching. Ανεξονται (*anexontai*, "tolerate") is used with the strong negative ουκ (ouk) to show a deliberate non-toleration of healthy teaching and instead a distinct preference for unhealthy choices.

This raises the question of motivation. Why do they avoid healthy teaching? Paul describes that motivation with the word for "runaway desire," επιθυμιας (epithumias). Because of this self-focused desire, a man or woman will have ears that itch. He uses the word *kneth*, which means "to itch or tickle;" therefore, they will turn away from listening to truth and wander into the realms of myth. Here, the term (NRSV "wandering," NIV "turn aside") is εκτρεπω (ektrepo), εκτραπη (ektrape), literally "to take a route away from the pathway." Timothy must be ready to encounter people who have (intentionally or unintentionally) avoided healthy teaching in favor of myths that support their own present desires. As a teacher, Timothy will deal not only with an audience that avoids healthy truth, but one that has instead a set of preferred myths that will support the behaviors that their desires have led them to embrace. The nature of a myth is that it supplies mythic promises of success, which then become an energizing part of the ideological package.

The presence of a fully formed mythic framework makes Timothy's teaching task more complicated and difficult, except when the sheer weight of wrongness and falsity within the myth begins to fall apart and collapse on its own unbalanced weight—or lack of weight. When that collapse begins to happen, then it is possible for the teacher of a more truthful way to break through the shell of isolating self-desire and intellectual/ethical/spiritual preoccupation that the myths have supported.

C.S. Lewis recognized this moment when truth can break through in his remarkably wise book, Miracles. He concludes his chapter on the Grand Miracle, which is the fact of the coming of Jesus Christ, with this paragraph:

> With this our sketch of the Grand Miracle may end. Its credibility does not lie in Obviousness.... The doctrine of the Incarnation works into our minds quite differently. It digs beneath the surface, works through the rest of our knowledge by unexpected channels, harmonises best with our deepest apprehensions and our 'second thoughts'.[13]

---

[13]C.S. Lewis, *Miracles* (New York: HarperCollins, 2001), 212.

Paul urges Timothy to stay his course, to keep his mind healthy, to take in stride the hardships; but best of all, Timothy is called to do the work of a welcomer. He is to invite men and women into the place of good news, which means to invite every listener farther in and farther up to the place of a larger hope, a hope that they may not yet have experienced or even dreamed of, the place of second thoughts.

Finally, the older Paul says to the younger Timothy, "fulfill your ministry." Be who you are, where you are, as one who has discovered God's love and is set free to share it.

II Timothy 4:6-8 As for me, I am already being poured out as a libation, and the time of my departure has come. I have fought the good fight, I have finished the race, I have kept the faith. From now on there is reserved for me the crown of righteousness, which the Lord, the righteous judge, will give me on that day, and not only to me but also to all who have longed for his appearing.

The word Paul uses to describe what is happening to him in his present place and time is σπενδομαι ("to pour out"), *spendomai*. The King James translates the word "offered." The NRSV translates it "being poured out as a libation."

He then says, "My season, my decisive hour has come for me." καιρος (kairos) is the word he uses here. This is not so much a chronological term as it is a dramatic moment, an important moment in his life. "I have fought the good fight;" his word for "good" is καλον (kalon), which means "excellent, competent." It is the word Jesus uses when he describes himself as the "good shepherd" in John 10—the excellent shepherd, who does not lose his sheep.

Now Paul uses the same word in the same way. He means that he has not sought to evade the hardship and battles that were in his path. He did not seek them, either—but when they came, he took them head-on. Similarly, an excellent shepherd does not arrange for the sheep to run away from the fold—but when they do, the good shepherd does his best to find them. He does what needs to be done. This is the spirit of Paul's reference to the battles fought. "When they come, I do my best to be a competent warrior." Then he changes the scene from that of the warrior to that of the athlete, one who runs a race to the ribbon. Paul does not call himself the winner of his race, since the track judge actually sees the runner break the ribbon at that key moment and calls the race, and only the field judge makes that announcement. But we do hear that Paul is to be awarded a medal; therefore, he has crossed the finish line where the ribbon has been.

Paul has kept the faith; he has trusted God the whole way, which is the sense of that statement. Therefore, there is a crown for Paul. (The word στεφανος, *stephanos*, describes an athlete's crown of laurel leaves—not the crown, *diadem*, that a king would wear.) Paul is announcing that he has won a medal of bronze or silver or gold, which recognizes the finishing of a race in a time that the scorekeeper notices and records in the book. Paul calls his award "the crown of righteousness." The word δικαιους, when it refers to God, is usually translated in the English text by the word "righteousness." When it refers to our experience, it is translated "justification."

Paul claims this good gift from God, not for himself alone in his race, but for all who have run their own race toward the goal of the Lord of the track—who is the starter of the race and who is, thankfully, the final scorekeeper.

II Timothy 4:9-15 Do your best to come to me soon, for Demas, in love with this present world, has deserted me and gone to Thessalonica; Crescens has gone to Galatia, Titus to Dalmatia. Only Luke is with me. Get Mark and bring him with you, for he is useful in my ministry. I have sent Tychicus to Ephesus. When you come, bring the cloak that I left with

Carpus at Troas, also the books, and above all the parchments. Alexander the coppersmith did me great harm; the Lord will pay him back for his deeds. You also must beware of him, for he strongly opposed our message.

The final words of II Timothy are personal in every way. Paul has favors to ask; he includes last-minute advice; he tells about people in his life, and best of all he continues to share his faith. In their own way, the words of Paul become helpful teaching for those of us who read this letter many years later.

He hopes that Timothy can speed up his travel plans, since several of their teammates are no longer nearby. Demas is noted first. We know of him from Colossians 4:14 and Philemon 24. From those prison letters, written earlier by Paul, we know that Demas was then actually with Paul. As pressures have intensified, he has left for his home city of Thessalonica. Timothy would know him from that city, where Timothy had spent time, or from Ephesus, where Demas also had friends. Out of fear for his own safety, Demas has left Paul. Paul mentions Demas first, which would imply that because he was especially known to Timothy, Timothy needs to know what has happened—perhaps so that he can find Demas when he travels through Thessalonica, which is on the major route from the province of Asia, through Macedonia and on to the port near Corinth. Perhaps Thessalonica was Demas's original home. We know from Acts 17 that Timothy had a role to play in that city earlier. Crescens is also mentioned in connection with his trip to Galatia, which is a province well known to Timothy.

Titus was a disciple with whom Paul also worked very closely, as we know from a letter Paul wrote to Titus. Titus, like Timothy, was a Greek won to Christ. We know of his important role with the Corinthian church because his name appears in II Corinthians 18. He was earlier entrusted by Paul to visit Corinth. "We are sending the brother who is famous among all the churches..." (II Cor. 8:18). Titus is now underway to Dalmatia, which is in the northern part of the Adriatic coastline near modern-day Bosnia and Croatia. This is probably a missionary journey for Titus.

Presently Paul tells Timothy that the beloved physician Luke is the only one actually nearby in this time of his harshest imprisonment. He urges Timothy to bring Mark with him on the journey. Mark is also noted by Paul in the earlier letter to Colossians (4:10) and Philemon 23. It is possible Mark carried the letters to Philemon, Ephesus and Colossae. Now he is in Ephesus, and Paul hopes he can come on the long journey to Rome with Timothy. They may be about the same age. Mark had been with

Peter and also Barnabas; at the very first of the journeys from Antioch, Paul had been critical of Mark—but that breach of friendship is now healed, as we can tell from the Colossian and Philemon letters. Paul wants these two younger men, Timothy and Mark, to travel together. Paul highly respects the stature and ministry of Mark, just as he respects Timothy. I wonder if Paul is aware that Mark is writing a narrative of the life of Jesus, which we and all the world will treasure as the Gospel of Mark. Tychius we know more about through other letters, and he has been sent by Paul to Ephesus. Does he carry Paul's letter to the Ephesians? See Ephesians 6:21-22. He is also mentioned in a companion letter to the Colossians (see Colossians 4:7). Tychius is also mentioned by Paul in his letter to Titus, as one who will probably be sent to Crete (Titus 3:12). He also traveled with Trophimus and Paul to Jerusalem (Acts 20:4).

Paul knows that Timothy will travel through Troas in order to sail across the Aegean Sea, so he asks a clothing-and-book favor. "Bring the cloak I left with Carpus, the books, and the parchments." He then alerts Timothy to dangers at Troas. "Alexander the coppersmith did me great harm." He doesn't ask Timothy to set up a revenge hit, but he insists on moderation on Timothy's part. "Don't worry, Timothy, the Lord is the one who is judge and jury. Leave the enactment of whatever repayment is needed to the Lord." But having given this advice, Paul counsels Timothy to keep his eyes open and to be streetwise. "You must beware of him...." Paul keeps track of people, and even Alexander should be grateful that his name is mentioned in a Pauline letter but not singled out for revenge. This Alexander is probably not the Alexander mentioned in I Timothy 1:20. Paul, in a simple indicative way of writing, simply tells the truth. He advises Timothy to exercise restraint, but to keep his eyes wide open and stay alert so that he can safely navigate a city like Troas.

II Timothy 4:16-22 At my first defense no one came to my support, but all deserted me. May it not be counted against them! But the Lord stood by me and gave me strength, so that through me the message might be fully proclaimed and all the Gentiles might hear it. So I was rescued from the lion's mouth. The Lord will rescue me from every evil attack and save me for his heavenly kingdom. To him be the glory forever and ever. Amen. Greet Prisca and Aquila, and the household of Onesiphorus. Erastus remained in Corinth; Trophimus I left ill in Miletus. Do your best to come before winter. Eubulus sends greetings to you, as do Pudens and Linus and Claudia and all the brothers and sisters. The Lord be with your spirit. Grace be with you.

Paul tells of his trial before Praetorian prosecutors and judges. No one stood with him in that first hearing.

They all deserted him. Is this a reference to Demas, who left because of fear? Paul notes the fact, but without further comment, except that he prays for them: "May it not be counted against them." That Paul does not focus on his aloneness or feel sorry for himself is shown in his next sentence, "But the Lord stood by me and gave me strength...." He even hints that at his trial, the good news about Christ was made known to his Gentile judges and guards. But the big news that Paul can report to Timothy is that he was rescued from the lion's mouth.

We know from Tacitus that in the arena, condemned people were thrown onto the arena surface, where lions killed them as entertainment for Roman citizens. It is this terrible punishment that many believers faced in the arena. According to Clement's letter to the Corinthians later in the century, that punishment is what finally happened to the great Apostle Paul. But not yet! He is able to complete his book. We hope that Timothy managed to arrive in Rome before winter, with the coat and the books too.

His final greetings are written in his own hand, and Paul himself tells of this. It is a signature pattern that he employs in all his letters. We know that because of his final words to the Galatians (Gal. 6:11), and in II

Thessalonians 3:17 he writes, "I, Paul, write this greeting with my own hand. This is the mark in every letter of mine."

He greets his two favorite friends who now are living in Ephesus, Prisca and Aquila, then Onesiphorus. He relates that Erastus is still in Corinth. Erastus is mentioned in Romans as a city official. In Acts 19:22, after the riot at Ephesus, Paul sent Timothy and Erastus to Macedonia while Paul stayed on in Asia—and then along with Trophimus and Tychus, Paul made his major trip to Jerusalem. Now Trophimus is ill at Miletus, a few miles south of Ephesus. Paul's last request of Timothy is about the winter that lies ahead: "Do your best to come before winter."

There are four more names in the letter. One is Eubulus, a companion of Paul's. He is probably the secretary with whose help Paul is writing the letter. The other names are unknown to us, but they may be fellow prisoners: Linus, Pudens, and Claudia. His last words in the letter surround a double use of the preposition "with." The Lord be "with" your spirit; and then the great surprise love word of Paul, grace be "with" you.

Paul is a man in Christ, a man who loves people, ordinary people. The Lord and people are on his heart from start to finish. His final words are his prayer for one young man named Timothy: "The Lord be with you, Timothy, and may you rest in his love for you." To the point, simple, and unforgettable—like the man who wrote the words, and even more so like his Lord.

Afterword

Those of us who study the text of the Holy Bible have the benefit of interpretive scholarship that spans the long history of enquiry into the world and the words of ancient biblical manuscripts. We have the resources of the rabbis who wrote commentaries on the Old Testament law and the prophets. One of the major gifts for the study of the Bible was found in the caves near the Dead Sea in 1946, the Dead Sea Scrolls. The Talmud of Rabbi Hillel is also an example of the tradition, deeply embedded in Jewish history, of commentary on the theological meaning and ethical importance of biblical texts.

From the church fathers in the early centuries of the Christian era, that tradition of commentary has continued. One of the leading modern authorities on Bible texts, Professor Bruce Metzger, is the editor of the New RSV Oxford Annotated Bible. Professor Metzger has noted that even if we had no Greek manuscripts of the New Testament, we would be able to construct an entire New Testament out of texts quoted by those very Church fathers in the Western and Eastern Churches. For us who live today in the English-speaking world, we have a rich collection of translations of the Bible in the English language. Serious Bible study should always begin with these English texts. In them we are able to watch how translators of Hebrew and Greek manuscripts have endeavored to offer the best sense of the original writers in the language we understand.

Bible study always begins with the text itself and then moves forward, by simple inductive questions, from what a writer or speaker says to what the writer or speaker means. This journey from "words understood" to content as "meaning understood" invites a reader to wonder about the cultural and spiritual atmosphere of events that were contemporary with the time of the writer. Because each reader must make this necessary journey, it is important to examine the cultural and historical settings of the events and teachings that confront us as we read the words of the Bible.

Within this commentary on II Timothy, I have endeavored to take this journey with you, the reader. Many interpretations, from the earliest to the most recent, have informed that journey for me. What follows now is a limited bibliography of sources that have in different ways been with me as partners through that journey.

First, I will honor several theological interpreters who have been very important teachers for me. Karl Barth is one decisive influence. His lecture series at the University of Bonn after WWII, now published in his book Dogmatics in Outline, is his commentary on the Apostles Creed and a brilliant introduction to his theology. Barth also was the principal writer of the 1934 faith affirmation, The Barmen Declaration. As a biblical interpreter, his commentaries on Romans and Philippians have both deeply blessed me. His young friend Dietrich Bonhoeffer has also been a strong influence in helping me understand the dark challenges of Gnosticism; the challenge Paul faced in its early appearance was not unlike what Bonhoeffer faced in the folk philosophy of the German Third Reich's radical theories in the 1930s. Bonhoeffer's Cost of Discipleship is the most exciting exposition of the Sermon on the Mount in the twentieth century. John R.W. Stott has been my steady influence regarding the basic importance of Christ-centeredness. This he joined with a moderation of method that protects those whom he has taught from the extremes of specialized interpretation. C.S. Lewis is noted in several places in this commentary, because of his understanding of the power of goodness over against the power of evil. His Mere Christianity theme was also profoundly expressed in the first century by St. Paul in II Timothy. I appreciate Helmut Thielicke and Barth, along with John Calvin and Martin Luther, for their insistence on the primacy of biblical theology, with its faithful attention to the biblical texts, as the primary theological task before making the necessary deductions and syntheses that are needed for systematic theology. This insistence in their theology echoes the insistence of St. Paul in his advice to Timothy, to trust the healthy truth of the texts in Scripture. At the end of the day, they will outlast the unhealthy falseness of the grand myths of our own preferences and ethical desires.

I also owe a debt to the Russian writers Solzhenitsyn, Agursky, and Barabanov, who in their book *From Under the Rubble* discuss the important need for Christian believers to recognize our own ambiguity—and therefore our own need for the checks and balances upon ourselves that are present in the gospel of law and grace.

Each of these writers has been a companion in my mind to the man from Tarsus, who wrote a brief letter of only four chapters to a disciple of Jesus named Timothy.

Let me also list technical interpreters and research scholars who have aided me during this study. Some I have found to be soul mates, and some others I have studied, but though I learned from them I did not decide to follow their interpretive way.

BIBLIOGRAPHY

Albright, William F. *Recent Discoveries in Bible Lands.*
New York: Funk & Wagnalls, 1955.

Barrett, C.K. *The Pastoral Epistles: In the New English Bible.* Edited by H.F.D Sparks. Oxford: Clarendon Press, 1963. I appreciate Barrett for his commentary, but I do not agree with his authorship assessment.

Barth, Karl. *Dogmatics in Outline.* New York: Harper & Row, 1959.

Bonhoeffer, Dietrich. *Cost of Discipleship.* New York: Touchstone, 1995.

Boswell, James. *The Life of Samuel Johnson.* Herts, UK: Wordsworth Editions, 2008.

Bruce, F.F. *New Testament History.* London: Thomas Nelson, 1969. The careful and exacting scholarship of F.F. Bruce is always helpful in the interpretation of New Testament documents. He holds to the Pauline authorship of II Timothy.

Calvin, John. *1, 2 Timothy and Titus.* Edited by Alister McGrath and J.I. Packer. Wheaton, IL: Crossway, 1998. Calvin agrees with the Church Fathers in their confidence in Paul as the author of the Pastoral Letters.

------. *Institutes of the Christian Religion.* Grand Rapids, Baker: 1987.

Chrysostom, John. "Homilies on II Timothy" in *Colossians, 1-2 Thessalonians, 1-2 Timothy, Titus, Philemon*. Vol. 9 of *Ancient Christian Commentary on Scripture: New Testament*. Edited by Peter Gorday. Downers Grove, IL: InterVarsity Press, 2000.

Confessional Synod of the German Evangelical Church. The Theological Declaration of Barmen. Barmen, Germany, May 29-31, 1934. Accessed June 3, 2014. https://www.pcusa.org/media/uploads/oga/pdf/boc.pdf.

Coogan, Michael, ed. *Oxford History of the Biblical World*. New York: Oxford University Press, 1998. This is a very helpful historical overview of the first-century period. See also Bruce, F.F. *New Testament History*. London: Thomas Nelson, 1969; and Jeremias, Joachim. *Jerusalem in the Time of Jesus*. Minneapolis: Fortress Press, 1969.

Dostoevsky, Fyodor. *The Karamazov Brothers*. Translated by Ignat Avsey. New York: Oxford University Press, 1994.

Earle, Ralph H. *The Expositor's Bible Commentary: Ephesians through Philemon*. Grand Rapids: Zondervan, 1978.

Finegan, Jack. *Handbook of Biblical Chronology: Principles of Time Reckoning in the Ancient World and Problems of Chronology in the Bible.* Princeton, NJ: Princeton University Press, 1964. His work is always helpful.

Fiore, Benjamin. *Pastoral Epistles: First Timothy, Second Timothy, and Titus.* Vol. 12 of *Sacra Pagina Series.* Edited by Daniel J. Harrington. Collegeville, MN: Liturgical Press, 2007. Fiore holds to a pseudonymous authorship. His arguments are weakened by his inability to explain the highly personal element in the text.

Grant, Frederick C. *Nelson's Bible Commentary: New Testament, Romans-Revelation.* Vol. 7 of *Nelson's Bible Commentary.* New York: Nelson, 1962. Grant has collected numerous historical markers that are not very helpful.

Hanson, Anthony Tyrrell. *Studies in the Pastoral Epistles.* London: SPCK, 1968. Hanson argues for an authorship date of 125 CE and a source other than Paul. He has no evidence to produce, except for Marcion's repudiation of the Pastoral Letters.

Johnson, Luke Timothy. *The First and Second Letters to Timothy.* Vol. 35A of *The Anchor Bible Commentaries.* New York: Doubleday, 1999. This Yale Divinity School New Testament scholar has written one of the most even handed of all recent commentaries. He argues for Paul's authorship with a brilliant grasp of the whole range of scholarly research.

Josipovici, Gabriel D. *The Book of God: A Response to the Bible.* New Haven, CT: Yale University Press, 1988. A brilliant interpreter of the first five books of the Old Testament and a wise critic of document deconstructionists.

Kleist, James A., ed. *The Epistles of St. Clement of Rome and St. Ignatius of Antioch.* Vol. 1 of *Ancient Christian Writers.* New York: Newman Press, 1946.

Leaney, A.R.C. *The Epistles to Timothy, Titus, and Philemon: Introduction and Commentary.* London: SCM, 1960. He argues for a sincere Paulinist writer at a later date. His method is not convincing, as he picks and chooses his way through II Timothy.

Lewis, C.S. *An Experiment in Criticism.* Cambridge: Cambridge University Press, 1973.

------. *Miracles.* New York: HarperCollins, 2001.

------. *The Weight of Glory.* New York: HarperCollins, 2001.

Martin, Ralph P. *Philippians.* Vol. 11 of *The Tyndale New Testament Commentaries.* Wheaton, IL: IVP, 2007. Argues for Pauline authorship.

Mounce, William D. *Pastoral Epistles.* Vol. 46 of *Word Biblical Commentary.* Nashville: Thomas Nelson, 2000. helpful in actually enabling a reader to see the relevance of the text to present life. This interpretation skillfully challenges the objections of the pseudo-

Pauline authorship group using the latest manuscript archeological evidence. He argues for Pauline authorship.

Pascal, Blaise. *Pensees: Thoughts on Religion and Other Subjects*. Edited by H.S. Thayer and Elisabeth B. Thayer. Translated by William Finlayson Trotter. New York: Washington Square Press, 1965.

Ricoeur, Paul. *Essays on Biblical Interpretation*. Edited by Lewis S. Mudge. Minneapolis: Fortress Press, 1980. Also Dibelius, Martin, and Hans Conzelmann. *The Pastoral Epistles: A Commentary on the Epistles*. Vols. 68-70 of *Hermeneia; A Critical and Historical Commentary on the Bible*. Minneapolis: Fortress, 1972. These interpreters see the pastorals as later books, written reverently by Christians who idealized how Paul would have written to the young Church. These later writers thus make Paul a chief witness for orthodoxy against Marcion.

Stott, John R.W. *The Story of the New Testament: Men with a Message*. Grand Rapids: Baker Books, 2001.

------. *The Message of Acts: The Bible Speaks Today Series*. Downers Grove: IVP, 1994. Stott is the most helpful in actually enabling a reader to see the relevance of the text to present life.

CPSIA information can be obtained at www.ICGtesting.com
Printed in the USA
BVOW04s1926041114

373663BV00001B/2/P